FTCE General Knowledge
Practice Test Kit
Teacher Certification Exam

By: Sharon Wynne, M.S.

XAMonline, Inc.
Boston

Copyright © 2014 XAMonline, Inc.
All rights reserved. No part of the material protected by this copyright notice may be reproduced or utilized in any form or by any means, electronic or mechanical, including photocopying, recording or by any information storage and retrievable system, without written permission from the copyright holder.

To obtain permission(s) to use the material from this work for any purpose including workshops or seminars, please submit a written request to:

XAMonline, Inc.
21 Orient Avenue
Melrose, MA 02176
Email: info@xamonline.com
Web: www.xamonline.com
Phone: 1-800-301-4647
Fax: 617-583-5552

Library of Congress Cataloging-in-Publication Data

Wynne, Sharon A.
FTCE General Knowledge Practice Test Kit: Teacher Certification /
Sharon A. Wynne 1st edition   ISBN 978-1-60787-360-0
1. FTCE General Knowledge Test   2. Study Guides.   3. FTCE
4. Teachers' Certification & Licensure   5. Careers

Disclaimer:
The opinions expressed in this publication are the sole works of XAMonline and were created independently from the State Department of Education or other testing affiliates.

Sample test questions are developed by XAMonline and are not former tests. XAMonline makes no claims nor guarantees teacher candidates a passing score.

Printed in the United States of America
FTCE General Knowledge Practice Test Kit
ISBN: 978-1-60787-360-0

Table of Contents

English Pretest **1**

Answer Key 13

Rigor Table 14

Rationales 15

Math Pretest **38**

Answer Key 49

Rigor Table 50

Rationales 51

Reading Pretest **78**

Answer Key 91

Rigor Table 92

Rationales 93

English Posttest **114**

Answer Key 126

Rigor Table 127

Rationales 128

Math Posttest **148**

Answer Key 158

Rigor Table 159

Rationales 160

Reading Posttest **185**

Answer Key 198

Rigor Table 199

Rationales 200

Test Format and Sample Questions
The FTCE General Knowledge Test consists of four subtests: English Language Skills, Mathematics, Reading, and Essay.

The Essay
For your essay, you will choose between two topics. The 50 minutes allotted for this section of the exam includes time to prepare, write, and edit your essay.

Your work will be scored holistically by two judges. The personal views you express will not be an issue. However, the skill with which you express those views, the logic of your arguments, and the degree to which you support your position will be very important in the scoring. Your essay will be scored both on substance and on the composition skills demonstrated.

Multiple-Choice Subtests
The English Language Skills and Reading subtests are each 40 minutes long and consist of approximately 40 multiple-choice questions per subtest. The Mathematics Subtest consists of approximately 45 multiple-choice questions and is 100 minutes long. Each multiple-choice subtest may also contain approximately 5 experimental items that will not be scored.

Each multiple-choice question will contain from two to four response options, and you will indicate your answer by selecting A, B, C, or D.

For the Mathematics Subtest, the test center will provide a 4-function calculator and a mathematics reference sheet.

Please note: The sample test questions in this Practice Test Kit include rigor level (Easy, Average, Rigorous) and the FTCE competency and skill (e.g., Skill 1.2) in parentheses right after each question.

English Pretest

DIRECTIONS: The passage below contains several errors. Read the passage. Then answer each test item by choosing the option that corrects an error in the underlined portion(s). No more than one underlined error will appear in each item. If no error exists, choose "No change is necessary."

If you give me ten dollars, I'll give you fifty in return. Does this sound too good to be true? Well, anything that sounds too good to be true probably is. That stands true for herbal supplements. Herbal supplements are main targeted toward improving one type of ailment. There is no cure-all herbal supplement so don't believe what he tells you. Herbal supplement can fix more than one thing.

    Herbal supplements is great and have a lot of positive things to offer its takers and have become very popular with consumers. Many doctors are even suggesting that they try natural herbal remedies before prescribing an over-the-counter medication. Herbal supplements have given consumers a new power to self-diagnose and consumers can head to the health food store and pick up an herbal supplement rather than heading to the doctor. Herbal supplements take a little long than prescribed medication to clear up any illnesses, but they are a more natural way to go, and some consumers prefer that form of medication.

1. Herbal supplements are <u>main</u> targeted <u>toward</u> <u>improving</u> one type of ailment.
(Average) (Skill 4.8)

   A. mainly

   B. towards

   C. improve

   D. No change is necessary

2. There is <u>no</u> cure-all herbal <u>supplement</u> so don't believe what <u>he tells you</u>.
(Easy) (Skill 4.5)

   A. nothing

   B. supplemental

   C. you hear

   D. No change is necessary

3. Many doctors <u>are</u> even suggesting that <u>they</u> try natural herbal remedies before <u>prescribing</u> an over-the-counter medication.
(Rigorous) (Skill 4.4)

   A. is

   B. their patients

   C. prescribing,

   D. No change is necessary

4. **Herbal supplements <u>is</u> great and have <u>a lot</u> of positive things to offer <u>its</u> takers and have become very popular with consumers.**
(Easy) (Skill 4.3)

   A. are

   B. alot

   C. it's

   D. No change is necessary

5. **Herbal supplements take a little <u>long</u> than <u>prescribed</u> medication to clear up any illnesses, but they are a more natural way to go, and some consumers prefer that form of medication.**
(Average) (Skill 4.9)

   A. longer

   B. then

   C. perscribed

   D. No change is necessary

6. **Herbal <u>supplements</u> take a little long than prescribed <u>medication</u> to clear up any illnesses, but they are a <u>more natural</u> way to go, and some consumers prefer that form of medication.**
(Rigorous) (Skill 4.9)

   A. supplement

   B. medications

   C. more naturally

   D. No change is necessary

7. **Herbal <u>supplement</u> can fix more <u>than</u> one <u>thing</u>.**
(Average) (Skill 2.1)

   A. supplements

   B. then

   C. things

   D. No change is necessary

DIRECTIONS: The passage below contains several errors. Read the passage. Then answer each test item by choosing the option that corrects an error in the underlined portion(s). No more than one underlined error will appear in each item. If no error exists, choose "No change is necessary."

Bingo has many purposes in the United States. It is used as a learning and entertainment tool for children. Bingo is used as an entertainment tool for parties and picnics to entertain a large number of people easily and quickly. Bingo is also a common game played among elderly and church groups because of its simplistic way of entertaining.

    A typical bingo card has the word "bingo" printed across the top with columns of numbers inside boxes underneath. There is a "free" space located directly in the middle. There is usually one person who calls the numbers. For example, a ball or chip may be labeled "B12." Players then look under the "B" column for the number 12 and if it appears on his card, they place a marker on top of it. If there isn't a 12 under the letter "B" on a player's card, then they simply wait for the next number to be called.

8. <u>Players</u> then look under the "B" column for the number 12 and if it appears on <u>his</u> card, <u>they</u> place a marker on top of it.

   How should this sentence be rewritten?
   (Rigorous) (Skill 4.5)

   A. He

   B. their

   C. him

   D. No change is necessary

9. **Bingo is used as a learning and entertainment tool for children.**

   How should this sentence be rewritten?
   (Rigorous) (Skill 3.2)

   A. Bingo is used as a learning tool and entertainment for children.

   B. Bingo is used for learning and entertainment for children.

   C. Bingo is used to both teach and entertain children.

   D. No change is necessary

10. Players then look under the "B" column for the number 12 and if it appears on their card, they place a marker on top of it.
(Rigorous) (Skill 4.11)

   A. Players then look under the, "B" column for the number 12, and if it appears on their card they place a marker on top of it.

   B. Players then look under the "B" column for the number, 12, and if it appears on their card they place a marker on top of it.

   C. Players then look under the "B" column for the number 12 and if it appears on their card they place a marker on top of it.

   D. No change is necessary

DIRECTIONS: The passage below contains several errors. Read the passage. Then answer each test item by choosing the option that corrects an error in the underlined portion(s). No more than one underlined error will appear in each item. If no error exists, choose "No change is necessary."

A family of four, consisting of two children and two adults, were trying to decide where they should go to have lunch at. Each of them wanted something different, so deciding between four places was not an easy task. The youngest child wanted fast food of course simply because they wanted to get the toy prize of the week. The eldest child was watching her weight and wanted to skip lunch altogether. The Mother was in the mood for a nice deli sandwich, one with many layers of ham and cheese. The father wanted a nice juicy burger—but not the kind from a fast food establishment. After much minutes of deliberating, the family decided to simply return home for leftover chicken from the night before.

11. The **youngest** child wanted fast **food of course** simply because they **wanted** to get the toy prize of the week.
(Average) (Skill 4.11)

   A. young

   B. food, of course,

   C. want

   D. No change is necessary

4

12. The youngest child wanted fast food of course simply because they wanted to get the toy prize of the week.
    (Average) (Skill 4.4)

    A. children

    B. simple

    C. she

    D. No change is necessary

13. A family of four, consisting of two children and two adults, were trying to decide where they should go to have lunch at.
    (Rigorous) (Skill 3.1)

    A. four consisting

    B. deciding

    C. lunch.

    D. No change is necessary

14. Each of them wanted something different, so deciding between four places was not an easy task.
    (Rigorous) (Skill 2.2)

    A. One

    B. decided

    C. among

    D. No change is necessary

15. After much minutes of deliberating, the family decided to simply return home for leftover chicken from the night before.
    (Average) (Skill 4.8)

    A. many

    B. decides

    C. simple

    D. No change is necessary

16. The Mother was in the mood for a nice deli sandwich, one with many layers of ham and cheese.
    (Easy) (Skill 4.12)

    A. The mother

    B. much

    C. layer

    D. No change is necessary

DIRECTIONS: The passage below contains several errors. Read the passage. Then answer each test item by choosing the option that corrects an error in the underlined portion(s). No more than one underlined error will appear in each item. If no error exists, choose "No change is necessary."

California is known for many things. But do you know what dates back to 1874 when the gold minors invaded California? It's the tough as old boots, Levi's denim jeans. These jeans were originally made for the minors whom needed pants to withstand the rough terrain they often encountered. Levi Straus used heavy canvas fabric and brass ribbets in the seams to withstand the test of time. Not only are these jeans more tougher than any other denim jeans on the market for they are also very fashionable.

17. Not only are these jeans <u>more tougher than</u> any other denim jeans on the market for they are also very <u>fashionable</u>.
    (Average) (Skill 4.9)

    A. tougher

    B. then

    C. fashionible

    D. No change is necessary

18. <u>California</u> is known for <u>many things</u>.
    (Easy) (Skill 4.11)

    A. California, is known...

    B. much

    C. things!

    D. No change is necessary

19. These jeans were <u>originally</u> made for the <u>minors whom</u> needed pants to withstand <u>the rough terrain</u> they often encountered.
    (Rigorous) (Skill 4.7)

    A. original

    B. miners who

    C. the rough terrain,

    D. No change is necessary.

20. **These jeans were originally made for the miners who needed pants to withstand the rough terrain they often encountered.**

    How should this sentence be rewritten?
    (Rigorous) (Skills 4.4 and 4.6)

    A. These jeans were originally made for the miners that needed pants to withstand the rough terrain. They often encountered.

    B. The miners needed jeans that could withstand the rough terrain they often encountered.

    C. These jeans were originally made for the rough terrain the miners needed.

    D. These jeans were originally made to withstand the rough terrain that the miners often encountered.

21. **Not only are these jeans tougher than any other denim jeans on the market for they are also very fashionable.**

    How should this sentence be rewritten?
    (Rigorous) (Skills 3.2 and 4.11)

    A. Not only are these jeans tougher than any other denim jeans on the market, for they are also very fashionable.

    B. Not only are these jeans tougher than any other denim jeans on the market but they are also more fashionable.

    C. Not only are these jeans tougher than any other denim jeans on the market, but they are also very fashionable.

    D. Not only, are these jeans tougher than any other denim jeans on the market, but, they are also very fashionable.

22. **What does the idiom "tough as old boots" mean in the sentence, "It's the tough as old boots, Levi's denim jeans"?**
    (Average) (Skill 2.1)

    A. Very rugged

    B. Made of leather

    C. As old as boots

    D. Worn out and old

23. Levi Straus used heavy canvas fabric and brass ribbets in the seams to withstand the test of time.

    Which word is used incorrectly in the sentence?
    (Easy) (Skills 1.3 and 4.10)

    A. heavy

    B. ribbets

    C. seams

    D. time

DIRECTIONS: The passage below contains several errors. Read the passage. Then answer each test item by choosing the option that corrects an error in the underlined portion(s). No more than one underlined error will appear in each item. If no error exists, choose "No change is necessary."

I can't hardly believe that Kings dominion is opening again for the season this week. This season should be much more excitable because of the introduction of the new roller coaster—the Intimidator 305. Not only is it the 15th roller coaster that the park has ejected, but it is also the tallest and most fast coaster on the East Coast. The attendees of the park are looking forward to riding the newer roller coaster, that was concluded on January 9, 2013.

24. Not only is it the 15th roller coaster that the park has erected, but it is also the <u>tallest</u> and <u>most fast</u> coaster on the <u>East Coast.</u>
    (Easy) (Skill 4.9)

    A. taller

    B. fastest

    C. East coast

    D. No change is necessary

25. The attendees of the park are looking forward to riding the newer roller coaster, that was concluded on January 9, 2013.
    (Average)(Skill 4.9)

    A. attendance

    B. were

    C. newest

    D. No change is necessary

26. The season should be much more excitable because of the introduction of the new roller coaster.
    (Average) (Skill 4.8)

    A. shouldn't be

    B. more

    C. exciting

    D. No change is necessary

27. The attendees of the park are looking forward to riding the newest roller coaster that was concluded on January 9, 2013.
    (Average) (Skills 1.3 and 2.1)

    A. looked

    B. completed

    C. January 9 2013

    D. No change is necessary

28. I can't hardly believe that Kings dominion is opening again for the season this week.
    (Easy) (Skill 4.1)

    A. can

    B. King's

    C. weekly

    D. No change is necessary

29. Not only is it the 15th roller coaster that the park has ejected, but it is also the tallest and most fast coaster on the East Coast.
    (Rigorous) (Skill 2.1)

    A. Not only,

    B. erected

    C. taller

    D. No change is necessary

30. This season should be much more excitable because of the introduction of the new roller coaster—the Intimidator 305.
    (Rigorous) (Skill 4.11)

    A. the new roller coaster, the Intimidator 305.

    B. the new roller coaster—the Intimidator 305?

    C. the new, roller coaster, the Intimidator 305.

    D. No change is necessary

31. **The attendees of the park are looking forward to riding the newest <u>roller coaster, that</u> was concluded on January 9, 2013.** *(Rigorous) (Skills 3.3 and 4.11)*

    A. roller, coaster that

    B. roller coaster that,

    C. roller coaster that

    D. No change is necessary

32. **I can hardly believe that <u>Kings dominion</u> is opening again for the season this week.** *(Average) (Skill 4.12)*

    A. King's dominion

    B. Kings Dominion

    C. kings dominion

    D. No change is necessary

DIRECTIONS: Read the following passage and answer the questions that follow.

It is a requirement that all parents volunteer two hours during the course of the season. Or an alternative was to pay $8 so you can have some high school students work a shift for you. Lots of parents liked this idea and will take advantage of the opportunity. Shifts run an hour long, and it is well worth it to pay the money so you don't miss your sons game.

33. **It is a requirement that all parents volunteer two hours during the course of the season.** *(Average) (Skill 4.1)*

    How should the above sentence be rewritten?

    A. It is a requirement of all parents volunteering two hours during the course of the season.

    B. It is required of all parents to volunteer for two hours during the course of the season.

    C. They require all parents to volunteer during the season.

    D. Requiring all parents to volunteer for two hours of the season.

34. **An alternative <u>was</u> to pay $8 so you can have some <u>high school</u> students work a shift for you.**

    Which of the following options corrects an error in one of the underlined portions above? *(Average) (Skill 4.2)*

    A. is

    B. High School

    C. High school

    D. No change is necessary

35. **Many parents liked this idea and will take advantage of the opportunity.**

    How should the sentence be rewritten?
    (Rigorous) (Skill 4.2)

    A. Many parent's liked this idea and took advantage of the opportunity.

    B. Many parents like this idea and take advantage of the opportunity.

    C. Many parents like this idea and took advantage of the opportunity.

    D. Many parents did like this idea and take advantage of the opportunity.

36. **Shifts run an hour long, and it is well worth it to pay the money so you don't miss your sons games.**

    Which of the following options corrects an error in one of the underlined portions above?
    (Average) (Skill 4.11)

    A. Shift's

    B. too

    C. son's

    D. No change is necessary

37. **Or an alternative was to pay $8 so you can have some high school students work a shift for you.**

    Which of the following options corrects an error in one of the underlined portions above?
    (Easy) (Skill 3.2)

    A. An

    B. high-school

    C. student's

    D. No change is necessary

38. **Mr. Patel respectfully submitted his resignation and had a new job.**

    Which of the following options corrects an error in the underlined portion above?
    (Average) (Skill 1.1)

    A. respectfully submitted his resignation and has

    B. respectfully submitted his resignation before accepting

    C. respectfully submitted his resignation because of

    D. respectfully submitted his resignation and had

DIRECTIONS: Read the following passage and answer the questions that follow.

Cats was one of the longest running musicals. It opened October 7, 1982, at the Winter Garden Theater in New York City. New York City is also known as Manhattan. The music, which has become very popular and well-known, was written by Andrew Lloyd Webber. He grew up in London, England. Perhaps the best-known hit was "Memory," which became popular worldwide and was recorded in more than twelve languages. The actual story is based on the book *Old Possum's Book of Practical Cats* written by T.S. Eliot, which is a series of children's poems.

39. **Which sentence in the passage is irrelevant?**
    (Rigorous) (Skill 1.2)

    A. *Cats* was one of the longest running musicals.

    B. It opened October 7, 1982 at the Winter Garden Theater.

    C. New York City is also known as Manhattan.

    D. The music is popular and well-known and was written by Andrew Lloyd Webber.

40. **Which sentence in the passage is irrelevant?**
    (Rigorous) (Skill 1.2)

    A. The music, which has become very popular and well-known, was written by Andrew Lloyd Webber.

    B. He grew up in London, England.

    C. Perhaps the best-known hit was "Memory," which became popular worldwide.

    D. The actual story is based on the book *Old Possum's Book of Practical Cats*.

Answer Key: English Pretest

1. A
2. C
3. B
4. A
5. A
6. B
7. A
8. B
9. C
10. D
11. B
12. C
13. C
14. C
15. A
16. A
17. A
18. D
19. B
20. D
21. C
22. A
23. B
24. B
25. C
26. C
27. B
28. A
29. B
30. D
31. C
32. B
33. B
34. A
35. B
36. C
37. A
38. C
39. C
40. B

Rigor Table: English Pretest

	Easy 20%	Average 40%	Rigorous 40%
Questions	2, 4, 16, 18, 23, 24, 28, 37	1, 5, 7, 11, 12, 15, 17, 22, 25, 26, 27, 32, 33, 34, 36, 38	3, 6, 8, 9, 10, 13, 14, 19, 20, 21, 29, 30, 31, 35, 39, 40

Pretest with Rationales: English

DIRECTIONS: The passage below contains many errors. Read the passage. Then, answer each test item by choosing the option that corrects an error in the underlined portion(s). No more than one underlined error will appear in each item. If no error exists, choose "No change is necessary."

If you give me ten dollars, I'll give you fifty in return. Does this sound too good to be true? Well, anything that sounds too good to be true probably is. That stands true for herbal supplements. Herbal supplements are main targeted toward improving one type of ailment. There is no cure-all herbal supplement so don't believe what he tells you. Herbal supplement can fix more than one thing.

    Herbal supplements is great and have a lot of positive things to offer its takers and have become very popular with consumers. Many doctors are even suggesting that they try natural herbal remedies before prescribing an over-the-counter medication. Herbal supplements have given consumers a new power to self-diagnose and consumers can head to the health food store and pick up an herbal supplement rather than heading to the doctor. Herbal supplements take a little long than prescribed medication to clear up any illnesses, but they are a more natural way to go, and some consumers prefer that form of medication.

1. **Herbal supplements are <u>main</u> targeted <u>toward</u> <u>improving</u> one type of ailment.**
   (Average) (Skill 4.8)

   A. mainly

   B. towards

   C. improve

   D. No change is necessary

Answer: A. mainly
Option B doesn't work because the correct form of the word is indeed "toward." The gerund "improving" is necessary in the sentence. Therefore, Option A, "mainly," is the correct adverb needed.

2. There is <u>no</u> cure-all herbal <u>supplement</u> so don't believe what <u>he tells you</u>.
   (Easy)(Skill 4.5)

   A.   nothing

   B.   supplemental

   C.   you hear

   D.   No change is necessary

Answer: C. you hear
As the sentence reads now, "he" is a pronoun that doesn't refer to anyone. Therefore, it shouldn't be used at all.

3. Many doctors <u>are</u> even suggesting that <u>they</u> try natural herbal remedies before <u>prescribing</u> an over-the-counter medication.
   (Rigorous) (Skill 4.4)

   A.   is

   B.   their patients

   C.   prescribing,

   D.   No change is necessary

Answer: B. their patients
The pronoun "they" is used incorrectly because it implies that the doctors should try natural herbal remedies. However, "they" is being used to take the place of their patients but has not been introduced prior to this point in the passage.

16

4. **Herbal supplements is great and have a lot of positive things to offer its takers and have become very popular with consumers.**
   (Easy) (Skill 4.3)

   A.   are

   B.   alot

   C.   it's

   D.   No change is necessary

Answer: A. are
The linking verb must agree with the word supplements which is plural. Therefore, the correct verb must be "are," not "is."

5. **Herbal supplements take a little long than prescribed medications to clear up any illnesses, but they are a more natural way to go, and some consumers prefer that form of medication.**
   (Average) (Skill 4.9)

   A.   longer

   B.   then

   C.   perscribed

   D.   No changes necessary

Answer: A. longer
The sentence is comparing two things—herbal supplements to prescribed medications. The comparative form of the adjective "long" needs to be used and should be "longer."

6. Herbal <u>supplements</u> take a little long than prescribed <u>medication</u> to clear up any illnesses, but they are a <u>more natural</u> way to go, and some consumers prefer that form of medication.
   (Rigorous) (Skill 4.9)

   A. supplement

   B. medications

   C. more naturally

   D. No change necessary

Answer: B. medications
Since the sentence begins talking about herbal supplements—plural—the comparison, prescribe medications, must be the same and be a plural too.

7. Herbal <u>supplement</u> can fix more <u>than</u> one <u>thing</u>.
   (Average) (Skill 2.1)

   A. supplements

   B. then

   C. things

   D. No change is necessary

Answer: A. supplements
The article talks about herbal supplements and therefore must agree at all times throughout the article. Option B is incorrect because then indicates that something happens next. "Than" is the correct word used in comparisons.

DIRECTIONS: The passage below contains many errors. Read the passage. Then, answer each test item by choosing the option that corrects an error in the underlined portion(s). No more than one underlined error will appear in each item. If no error exists, choose "No change is necessary."

Bingo has many purposes in the United States. It is used as a learning and entertainment tool for children. Bingo is used as an entertainment tool for parties and picnics to entertain a large number of people easily and quickly. Bingo is also a common game played among elderly and church groups because of its simplistic way of entertaining.

A typical bingo card has the word "bingo" printed across the top with columns of numbers inside boxes underneath. There is a "free" space located directly in the middle. There is usually one person who calls the numbers. For example, a ball or chip may be labeled "B12." Players then look under the "B" column for the number 12 and if it appears on their card, they place a marker on top of it. If there isn't a 12 under the letter "B" on a player's card, then they simply wait for the next number to be called.

8. <u>Players</u> then look under the "B" column for the number 12 and if it appears on <u>his</u> card, <u>they</u> place a marker on top of it.

    (Rigorous) (Skill 4.5)

    A.   He

    B.   their

    C.   him

    D.   No change is necessary.

Answer: B. their
The sentence begins with the plural word "player" and is followed by the plural word "they." Therefore, the possessive word "their" is needed rather than the singular word "he" or "him."

9. **Bingo is used as a learning and entertainment tool for children.**

   How should this sentence be rewritten?
   (Rigorous) (Skill 3.2)

   A. Bingo is used as a learning tool and entertainment for children.

   B. Bingo is used for learning and entertainment for children.

   C. Bingo is used to both teach and entertain children.

   D. No change is necessary

Answer: C. Bingo is used to both teach and entertain children.

The best answer is Option C because the correlative conjunction "both" is used, and there is a similar sentence structure on both sides of the word. In both options A and B, the words being compared do not have the same structure.

10. **Players then look under the "B" column for the number 12 and if it appears on their card, they place a marker on top of it.**

    How should this sentence be rewritten?
    (Rigorous) (Skill 4.11)

    A. Players then look under the, "B" column for the number 12, and if it appears on their card they place a marker on top of it.

    B. Players then look under the "B" column for the number, 12, and if it appears on their card they place a marker on top of it.

    C. Players then look under the "B" column for the number 12 and if it appears on their card they place a marker on top of it.

    D. No change necessary

Answer: D. No change necessary

The way that the original sentence is punctuated is the correct way to punctuate it. A comma needs to appear after "card," because it separates a dependent clause from an independent clause.

DIRECTIONS: The passage below contains many errors. Read the passage. Then, answer each test item by choosing the option that corrects an error in the underlined portion(s). No more than one underlined error will appear in each item. If no error exists, choose "No change is necessary."

A family of four, consisting of two children and two adults, were trying to decide where they should go to have lunch at. Each of them wanted something different, so deciding between four places was not an easy task. The youngest child wanted fast food of course simply because they wanted to get the toy prize of the week. The eldest child was watching her weight and wanted to skip lunch altogether. The Mother was in the mood for a nice deli sandwich, one with many layers of ham and cheese. The father wanted a nice juicy burger – but not the kind from a fast food establishment. After much minutes of deliberating, the family decided to simply return home for leftover chicken from the night before.

11. The <u>youngest</u> child wanted fast <u>food of course</u> simply because they <u>wanted</u> to get the toy prize of the week.
    (Average) (Skill 4.11)

    A. young

    B. food, of course,

    C. want

    D. No change is necessary

Answer: B. food, of course,
"Of course" is a clause that is added into the sentence, and therefore, requires commas on either side. The sentence could exist without the addition of the words "of course" and, therefore, needs that punctuation.

12. The youngest <u>child</u> wanted fast food of course <u>simply</u> because <u>they</u> wanted to get the toy prize of the week.
    (Average) (Skill 4.4)

    A.   children

    B.   simple

    C.   she

    D.   No change is necessary

Answer: C. she
The sentence begins by drawing attention to the youngest child. Therefore, the pronoun used must agree with the singular. "She" is needed rather than "they."

13. A family of <u>four, consisting</u> of two children and two adults, were trying to <u>decide</u> where they should go to have <u>lunch at.</u>
    (Rigorous) (Skill 3.1)

    A.   four consisting

    B.   deciding

    C.   lunch.

    D.   No change is necessary

Answer: C. lunch.
Sentences should not end with a preposition. The sentence should simply read, "...were trying to decide where they should go to have lunch."

14. **Each** of them wanted something different, so **deciding between** four places was not an easy task.
(Rigorous) (Skill 2.2)

   A.   One

   B.   decided

   C.   among

   D.   No change is necessary

Answer: C. among
In this case, you must use "among," as "between" should only be used when comparing two items.

15. After **much** minutes of deliberating, the family **decided** to **simply** return home for leftover chicken from the night before.
(Average) (Skill 4.8)

   A.   many

   B.   decides

   C.   simple

   D.   No change is necessary.

Answer: A. many
The word "many" is needed instead because the minutes could be counted as individual items as in, "How *many* minutes?" "Much" is used when an exact number cannot be determined. "How *much* detergent do I need to put in the washer?"

16. **The Mother was in the mood for a nice deli sandwich, one with many layers of ham and cheese.**
    (Easy) (Skill 4.12)

    A. The mother

    B. much

    C. layer

    D. No change is necessary

Answer: A. The mother
Only when words like mom or mother are used as names should they have a capital letter. For example, "I know, but Mom said I could wear this dress today." Mom is being used as a name and therefore requires a capital letter.

DIRECTIONS: The passage below contains many errors. Read the passage. Then, answer each test item by choosing the option that corrects an error in the underlined portion(s). No more than one underlined error will appear in each item. If no error exists, choose "No change is necessary."

California is known for many things. But do you know what dates back to 1874 when the gold minors invaded California? It's the tough as old boots, Levi's denim jeans. These jeans were originally made for the minors whom needed pants to withstand the rough terrain they often encountered. Levi Straus used heavy canvas fabric and brass ribbets in the seams to withstand the test of time. Not only are these jeans more tougher than any other denim jeans on the market for they are also very fashionable.

17. Not only are these jeans <u>more tougher</u> <u>than</u> any other denim jeans on the market for they are also very <u>fashionable</u>.
    (Average) (Skill 4.9)

    A.   tougher

    B.   then

    C.   fashionible

    D.   No change is necessary

Answer: A. tougher
The correct form of the word "more tough" is "tougher."

18. <u>California</u> is known for <u>many</u> <u>things</u>.
    (Easy) (Skill 4.11)

    A.   California, is known...

    B.   much

    C.   things!

    D.   No change is necessary

Answer: D. No change is necessary
The way this simple sentence is written is punctuated and written correctly.

19. These jeans were <u>originally</u> made for the <u>minors whom</u> needed pants to withstand <u>the rough terrain</u> they often encountered.
(Rigorous) (Skill 4.7)

   A.   original

   B.   miners who

   C.   the rough terrain,

   D.   No change is necessary

Answer: B. miners who
There are two errors in this section. "Miners" is spelled incorrectly, and the word "whom" is only used as a pronoun when it is replacing a noun. The word "whom" in this sentence is acting as a descriptor of the miners and therefore should be "who."

20. These jeans were originally made for the miners who needed pants to withstand the rough terrain they often encountered.

   How should this sentence be rewritten?
   (Rigorous) (Skills 4.4 and 4.6)

   A.   These jeans were originally made for the miners that needed pants to withstand the rough terrain. They often encountered.

   B.   The miners needed jeans that could withstand the rough terrain they often encountered.

   C.   These jeans were originally made for the rough terrain the miners needed.

   D.   These jeans were originally made to withstand the rough terrain that the miners often encountered.

Answer: D. These jeans were originally made to withstand the rough terrain that the miners often encountered.
In the original sentence, the pronoun "they" is not distinctly assigned and can represent either the miners or the jeans. Option D makes the idea much clearer and assigns the pronoun to the miners.

21. Not only are these jeans tougher than any other denim jeans on the market for they are also very fashionable.

    How should this sentence be rewritten?
    (Rigorous) (Skills 3.2, 4.11)

    A. Not only are these jeans tougher than any other denim jeans on the market, for they are also very fashionable.

    B. Not only are these jeans tougher than any other denim jeans on the market but they are also more fashionable.

    C. Not only are these jeans tougher than any other denim jeans on the market, but they are also very fashionable.

    D. Not only, are these jeans tougher than any other denim jeans on the market, but, they are also very fashionable.

Answer: C. Not only are these jeans tougher than any other denim jeans on the market, but they are also very fashionable.
The first part of the correlative conjunction *not only…but also* needs to be followed with "but" (instead of "for."), which serves as a conjunction. A comma is needed before a conjunction that joins two independent clauses.

22. What does the idiom "tough as old boots" mean in the sentence, "It's the tough as old boots, Levi's denim jeans"?
    (Average) (Skill 2.1)

    A. Very rugged

    B. Made of leather

    C. As old as boots

    D. Worn out and old

Answer: A. Very rugged
The saying "tough as old boots" means that they are sturdy and rugged. This expression is used to describe Levi's denim jeans.

23. Levi Straus used heavy canvas fabric and brass ribbets in the seams to withstand the test of time.

    Which word is used incorrectly in the sentence?
    (Easy) (Skills 1.3 and 4.10)

    A. heavy

    B. ribbets

    C. seams

    D. time

Answer: B. ribbets
The correct word that should have been used in the sentence is "rivets."

DIRECTIONS: The passage below contains several errors. Read the passage. Then answer each test item by choosing the option that corrects an error in the underlined portion(s). No more than one underlined error will appear in each item. If no error exists, choose "No change is necessary."

I can't hardly believe that Kings dominion is opening again for the season this week. This season should be much more excitable because of the introduction of the new roller coaster – the Intimidator 305. Not only is it the 15th roller coaster that the park has ejected, but it is also the tallest and most fast coaster on the East Coast. The attendees of the park are looking forward to riding the newer roller coaster, that was concluded on January 9, 2013.

24. Not only is it the 15th roller coaster that the park has erected, but it is also the <u>tallest</u> and <u>most fast</u> coaster on the <u>East Coast.</u>
    (Easy) (Skill 4.9)

    A. taller

    B. fastest

    C. East coast

    D. No change is necessary

Answer: B. fastest
The two adjectives must agree, and the adjective "tallest" is used first. Therefore, the comparative adjective to use would be "fastest."

25. The <u>attendees</u> of the park <u>are</u> looking forward to riding the <u>newer</u> roller coaster, that was concluded on January 9, 2013.
    (Average) (Skill 4.9)

    A. attendance

    B. were

    C. newest

    D. No change is necessary

Answer: C. newest
"Newer" could be used if only two items were being compared. However, the passage states that this is the 15th roller coaster that has been added. Therefore, "newest" would be the correct word to use.

26. The season <u>should be</u> <u>much more</u> <u>excitable</u> because of the introduction of the new roller coaster.
    (Average) (Skill 4.8)

    A. shouldn't be

    B. more

    C. exciting

    D. No change is necessary

Answer: C. exciting
"Excitable" is the wrong adjective needed to describe the new season. It should be much more exciting.

27. The attendees of the park are looking forward to riding the newest roller coaster that was concluded on January 9, 2013.
(Average) (Skills 1.3 and 2.1)

    A.   looked

    B.   completed

    C.   January 9 2013

    D.   No change is necessary

Answer: B. completed
"Concluded" is used with an idea. For example, the jury concluded that the defendant was guilty. When being used with an object, like a roller coaster, then the word "completed" is used.

28. I can't hardly believe that Kings dominion is opening again for the season this week.
(Easy) (Skill 4.1)

    A.   can

    B.   King's

    C.   weekly

    D.   No change is necessary

Answer: A. can
The way the sentence is written now, "I can't hardly believe," it contains a double negative. The correct way to say that is, "I can hardly believe..."

29. **Not only** is it the 15th roller coaster that the park has **ejected**, but it is also the **tallest** and most fast coaster on the East Coast.
    (Rigorous) (Skill 2.1)

    A.   Not only,

    B.   erected

    C.   taller

    D.   No change is necessary

Answer: B. erected
"Ejected" means forced out. "Erect" means to put something upright. The wrong word was used in the paragraph.

30. This season should be much more excitable because of the introduction of the **new roller coaster—the Intimidator 305.**
    (Rigorous) (Skill 4.11)

    A.   the new roller coaster, the Intimidator 305.

    B.   the new roller coaster – the Intimidator 305?

    C.   the new, roller coaster, the Intimidator 305.

    D.   No change is necessary

Answer: D. No change is necessary
A dash is an acceptable form of punctuation, and this is a great way to use one.

31. The attendees of the park are looking forward to riding the newest <u>roller coaster, that</u> was concluded on January 9, 2013.
    (Rigorous) (Skills 3.3 and 4.11)

    A.   roller, coaster that

    B.   roller coaster that,

    C.   roller coaster that

    D.   No change is necessary

Answer: C. roller coaster that
No comma is needed between "roller coaster" and "that" because there are two independent clauses being joined.

32. I can hardly believe that <u>Kings dominion</u> is opening again for the season this week.
    (Average) (Skill 4.12)

    A.   King's dominion

    B.   Kings Dominion

    C.   kings dominion

    D.   No change is necessary

Answer: B. Kings Dominion
Kings Dominion is the proper name of an amusement park. Therefore, both names must be capitalized.

DIRECTIONS: Read the following passage and answer the questions.

It is a requirement that all parents volunteer two hours during the course of the season. Or an alternative was to pay $8 so you can have some high school students work a shift for you. Lots of parents liked this idea and will take advantage of the opportunity. Shifts run an hour long, and it is well worth it to pay the money so you don't miss your sons game.

33. It is a requirement that all parents volunteer two hours during the course of the season.

How should the above sentence be rewritten?
(Average) (Skill 4.1)

    A.   It is a requirement of all parents volunteering two hours during the course of the season.

    B.   It is required of all parents to volunteer for two hours during the course of the season.

    C.   They require all parents to volunteer during the season.

    D.   Requiring all parents to volunteer for two hours of the season.

Answer: B. It is required of all parents to volunteer for two hours during the course of the season.
This is the only choice that works. Option C makes sense, but the pronoun "they" is not established and cannot be used in the first sentence of the paragraph.

34. An alternative <u>was</u> to pay $8 so you can have some <u>high school</u> students work a shift for you.

    Which of the following options corrects an error in one of the underlined portions above?
    (Average) (Skill 4.2)

    A.   is

    B.   High School

    C.   High school

    D.   No change is necessary.

Answer: A. is
The first sentence puts this passage in the present tense. Therefore, the verb tense must remain the same throughout the passage and "was" is a past tense verb.

35. Many parents liked this idea and will take advantage of the opportunity.

    How should the sentence be rewritten?
    (Rigorous) (Skill 4.2)

    A.   Many parent's liked this idea and took advantage of the opportunity.

    B.   Many parents like this idea and take advantage of the opportunity.

    C.   Many parents like this idea and took advantage of the opportunity.

    D.   Many parents did like this idea and take advantage of the opportunity.

Answer: B. Many parents like this idea and take advantage of the opportunity.
The verb tense between "like" and "take" must remain consistent in the sentence and consistent with the verb tense of the paragraph.

36. <u>Shifts</u> run an hour long, and it is well worth it <u>to</u> pay the money so you don't miss your <u>sons</u> games.

    Which of the following options corrects an error in one of the underlined portions above?
    (Average) (Skill 4.11)

    A. Shift's

    B. too

    C. son's

    D. No change is necessary

Answer: C. son's
"Son's game" is possessive. Therefore, an apostrophe is needed to show possession.

37. <u>Or an</u> alternative was to pay $8 so you can have some <u>high school students</u> work a shift for you.

    Which of the following options corrects an error in one of the underlined portions above?
    (Easy) (Skill 3.2)

    A. An

    B. high-school

    C. student's

    D. No change is necessary

Answer: A. An
"Or" is not needed to begin this sentence. The conjunction "or" should be used to join two clauses without the use of a period.

38. Mr. Patel respectfully submitted his resignation and had a new job.

Which of the following options corrects an error in one of the underlined portion above?
(Average) (Skill 1.1)

- A. respectfully submitted his resignation and has

- B. respectfully submitted his resignation before accepting

- C. respectfully submitted his resignation because of

- D. respectfully submitted his resignation and had

Answer: C. respectfully submitted his resignation because of
Option A eliminates any relationship of causality between submitting the resignation and having the new job. Option B just changes the sentence and, by omission, does not indicate the fact that Mr. Patel had a new job before submitting his resignation. Option D means that Mr. Patel first submitted his resignation and then got a new job.

DIRECTIONS: Read the passage below and answer the questions that follow.

Cats was one of the longest running musicals. It opened October 7, 1982, at the Winter Garden Theater in New York City. New York City is also known as Manhattan. The music, which has become very popular and well-known, was written by Andrew Lloyd Webber. He grew up in London, England. Perhaps the best-known hit was "Memory," which became popular worldwide and was recorded in more than twelve languages. The actual story is based on the book *Old Possum's Book of Practical Cats* written by T.S. Eliot, which is a series of children's poems.

39. **Which sentence in the passage is irrelevant?**
    (Rigorous) (Skill 1.2)

    A. *Cats* was one of the longest running musicals.

    B. It opened October 7, 1982 at the Winter Garden Theater.

    C. New York City is also known as Manhattan.

    D. The music is popular and well-known and was written by Andrew Lloyd Webber.

Answer: C. New York City is also known as Manhattan.
The idea that New York City is also known as Manhattan does not support the main idea of the passage. Therefore, it is irrelevant.

40. **Which sentence in the passage is irrelevant?**
    (Rigorous) (Skill 1.2)

    A. The music, which has become very popular and well-known, was written by Andrew Lloyd Webber.

    B. He grew up in London, England.

    C. Perhaps the best-known hit was "Memory," which became popular worldwide.

    D. The actual story is based on the book *Old Possum's Book of Practical Cats.*

Answer: B. He grew up in London, England.
The idea that Webber grew up in London, England, does not support the main idea of the passage. Therefore, it is irrelevant.

Mathematics Pretest

1. Which of the following is correct?
   (Easy) (Skill 5.1)

   A. 2,365 > 2,340

   B. 0.75 > 1.25

   C. 3/4 < 1/16

   D. -5 < -6

2. Simplify:

   $$\frac{5^{-2} \times 5^3}{5^5 \times 5^{-7}}$$

   (Average) (Skill 5.3)

   A. 5^5

   B. 125

   C. $\frac{1}{125}$

   D. 25

3. Choose the set in which the members are *not* equivalent.
   (Average) (Skill 5.1)

   A. 1/2, 0.5, 50%

   B. 10/5, 2.0, 200%

   C. 3/8, 0.385, 38.5%

   D. 7/10, 0.7, 70%

4. The digit 8 in the number 975.086 is in the:
   (Easy) (Skill 5.1)

   A. Tenths place

   B. Ones place

   C. Hundredths place

   D. Hundreds place

5. The relations given below demonstrate the following addition and multiplication property of real numbers:
   a + b = b + a
   ab = ba
   (Easy) (Skill 5.3)

   A. Commutative

   B. Associative

   C. Identity

   D. Inverse

6. $(3 \times 9)^4 =$
   (Rigorous) (Skill 5.4)

   A. $(3 \times 9)(3 \times 9)(27 \times 27)$

   B. $(3 \times 9) + (3 \times 9)$

   C. (12×36)

   D. $(3 \times 9) + (3 \times 9) + (3 \times 9) + (3 \times 9)$

7. At a publishing company, Mona can proofread 300 pages in 5 hours while Lisa can proofread 360 pages in 4 hours. If they share the task of proofreading a 375-page document, how long will it take them to complete the job?
   (Rigorous) (Skill 5.2)

   A. 2.5 hours

   B. 5 hours

   C. 3 hours

   D. 3.5 hours

8. A student had 60 days to appeal the results of an exam. If the results were received on March 23, what was the last day that the student could appeal?
   (Average) (Skill 5.2)

   A. May 21

   B. May 22

   C. May 23

   D. May 24

9. A coat is on sale for $135. If the discount offered is 25%, what was the original price of the coat?
   (Average) (Skill 5.2)

   A. $160

   B. $180

   C. $110

   D. $150

10. If three cups of concentrate are needed to make 2 gallons of fruit punch, how many cups are needed to make 5 gallons?
    (Average) (Skill 5.2)

    A. 6 cups

    B. 7 cups

    C. 7.5 cups

    D. 10 cups

11. A sofa sells for $520. If the retailer makes a 30% profit, what was the wholesale price? *(Average) (Skill 5.2)*

    A. $400

    B. $676

    C. $490

    D. $364

12. Kendra needs to paint one rectangular wall of her bedroom, which measures 18 feet by 10 feet. Each container of paint she will use can cover 15 square feet and costs $9.98. What is the best approximation for the total cost of the paint she will need? *(Rigorous) (Skill 6.5)*

    A. $120

    B. $180

    C. $240

    D. $270

13. Jason can run a distance of 50 yards in 6.5 seconds. At this rate, how many feet can he run in a time of 26 seconds? *(Average) (Skill 6.4)*

    A. 200

    B. 400

    C. 600

    D. 800

14. Solve for *x*:

    $3(5 + 3x) - 8 = 88$

    (Average) (Skill 8.3)

    A. 30

    B. 9

    C. 4.5

    D. 27

15. Solve for *x*:

    $|2x + 3| > 4$

    (Rigorous) (Skill 8.3)

    A. $-\frac{7}{2} > x > \frac{1}{2}$

    B. $-\frac{1}{2} > x > \frac{7}{2}$

    C. $x < \frac{7}{2}$ or $x < -\frac{1}{2}$

    D. $x < -\frac{7}{2}$ or $x > \frac{1}{2}$

16. You are helping students list the steps needed to solve the word problem:

    "Mr. Jones is 5 times as old as his son. Two years later he will be 4 times as old as his son. How old is Mr. Jones?"

    One of the students makes the following list:

    1. Assume Mr. Jones' son is x years old. Express Mr. Jones' age in terms of x.
    2. Write how old they will be two years later in terms of x.
    3. Solve the equation for x.
    4. Multiply the answer by 5 to get Mr. Jones' age.

    What step is missing between steps 2 and 3?
    (Rigorous) (Skill 8.2)

    A. Write an equation setting Mr. Jones' age equal to 5 times his son's age

    B. Write an equation setting Mr. Jones' age two years later equal to 5 times his son's age two years later

    C. Write an equation setting Mr. Jones' age equal to 4 times his son's age

    D. Write an equation setting Mr. Jones' age two years later equal to 4 times his son's age two years later

17. Which of the following points does *not* lie on the graph of $|y + 3| < |x - 3|$?
    (Rigorous) (Skill 8.2)

    A. (-5, 4)

    B. (-6, 0)

    C. (-3, -4)

    D. (7, 7)

18. What is the next term in the following sequence?

    {0.005, 0.03, 0.18, 1.08,... }

    (Rigorous) (Skill 8.1)

    A. 1.96

    B. 2.16

    C. 3.32

    D. 6.48

19. {1, 4, 7, 10, . . .}

    What is the 40th term in this sequence?
    (Easy) (Skill 8.1)

    A. 43

    B. 121

    C. 118

    D. 120

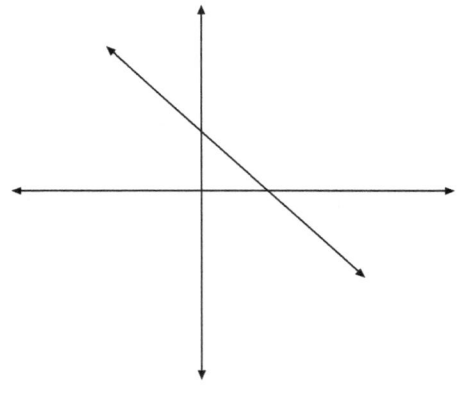

20. What is the x-intercept of the line represented by $4x + 2y = 12$?
    (Rigorous) (Skill 8.3)

    A. (0, 6)

    B. (3, 0)

    C. (0, 3)

    D. (0, 8)

21. A student has taken three tests in his algebra class for which the mean score is 88. He will take one more test and his final grade will be the mean of all four tests. He wants to achieve a final grade of 90. Which one of the following is the correct procedure to determine the score he needs on the fourth test?
    (Rigorous) (Skill 8.2)

    A. He needs a score 92 since (88 + 92) / 2 = 90.

    B. He needs a score of 89.5 since (88 + 90 + 90 + 90) / 4 = 89.5.

    C. He needs a score of 96 since (88 + 88 + 88 + 96) / 4 = 90.

    D. He cannot achieve a final grade of 90 since each of his scores on the first three tests is less than 90.

22. Which of the following shapes is *not* a parallelogram?
    (Easy) (Skill 7.1)

    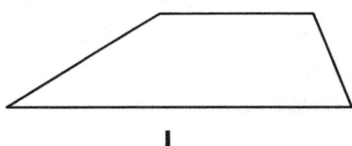

    I

    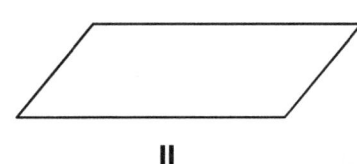

    II

    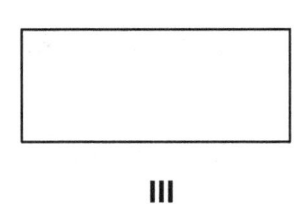

    III

    A. I and III

    B. II and III

    C. I only

    D. I, II, and III

23. An isosceles triangle has:
    (Easy) (Skill 7.1)

    A. Three equal sides

    B. Two equal sides

    C. No equal sides

    D. Two equal sides in some cases, no equal sides in others

24. Given similar polygons with corresponding sides of lengths 9 and 15, find the perimeter of the smaller polygon if the perimeter of the larger polygon is 150 units.
    (Average) (Skill 7.2)

    A. 54

    B. 135

    C. 90

    D. 126

25. Ginny and Nick head back to their respective colleges after being home for the weekend. They leave their house at the same time and drive for 4 hours. Ginny drives due south at the average rate of 60 miles per hour, and Nick drives due east at the average rate of 60 miles per hour. What is the straight-line distance between them, in miles, at the end of the 4 hours?
    (Rigorous) (Skill 7.2)

    A. $120\sqrt{2}$

    B. 240

    C. $240\sqrt{2}$

    D. 288

26. Given segment AC with B as its midpoint, find the coordinates of C if A = (5, 7) and B = (3, 6.5).
    (Rigorous) (Skill 7.3)

    A. (4, 6.5)

    B. (1, 6)

    C. (2, 0.5)

    D. (16, 1)

27. Which one of the following sets of points on a coordinate plane defines an isosceles right triangle?
    (Rigorous) (Skill 7.3)

    A. (4,0), (0,4), (4,4)

    B. (4,0), (0,6), (4,4)

    C. (0,0), (0,4), (5,2)

    D. (0,0), (5,0), (5,2)

28. The speed of light in space is about 3×10^8 meters per second. Express this in Kilometers per hour.
    (Rigorous) (Skill 6.2)

    A. 1.08×10^9 Km/hr

    B. 3.0×10^{11} Km/hr

    C. 1.08×10^{12} Km/hr

    D. 1.08×10^{15} Km/hr

29. Given a 30-meter x 60-meter garden with a circular fountain with a 5-meter radius, calculate the area of the portion of the garden *not* occupied by the fountain.
    (Rigorous) (Skill 6.1)

    A. 1,721 m²

    B. 1,879 m²

    C. 2,585 m²

    D. 1,015 m²

30. What is the length of a fourth of the circumference of a circle with a diameter of 24 cm?
    (Rigorous) (Skill 6.1)

    A. 18.85

    B. 75.4

    C. 32.45

    D. 20.75

31. What percentage of students got a C grade?
    (Average) (Skill 9.1)

    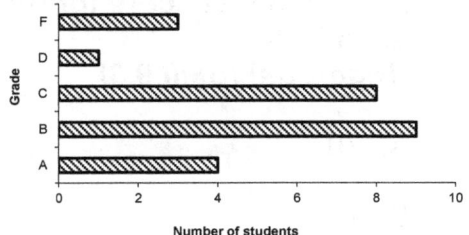

    A. 35

    B. 8

    C. 32

    D. 40

32. If George spends $300 per month on his utilities, how much does he spend during a two-month period for the combined total of his mortgage, food, and miscellaneous items?
    (Average) (Skill 9.1)

    A. $2,400

    B. $1,800

    C. $1,200

    D. $900

33. You are creating a pie chart to show the expenses for a business. If employee pay is 40% of the total expenditure, what central angle will you use to show that segment of the pie chart?
    (Average) (Skill 9.1)

    A. 72°

    B. 80°

    C. 40°

    D. 144°

34. **Which of the following is the most accurate inference that can be made from the graph shown below?**
(Average) (Skill 9.1)

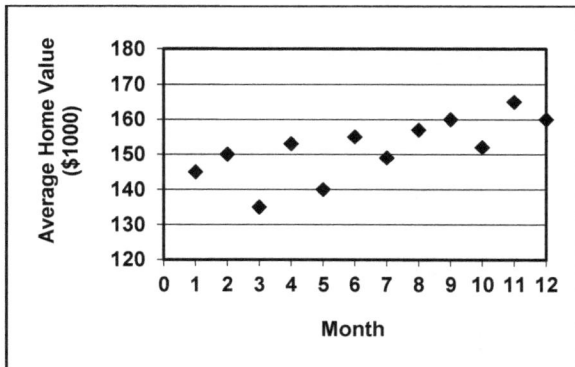

A. The average home value shows a decreasing trend over the 12-month period

B. The average home value shows an increasing trend over the 12-month period

C. The average home value stays about the same over the 12-month period

D. The data fluctuates too much to make any comment about the trend

35. **Melissa scores 60, 68, and 75 in the first three of five tests. What should her average score be for the last two tests so that her mean test score for the five tests is 70?**
(Rigorous) (Skill 9.3)

A. 70

B. 73.5

C. 75.5

D. 85

36. **Find the median of the following set of data:**

14 3 7 6 11 20

(Easy) (Skill 9.3)

A. 9

B. 8.5

C. 7

D. 11

37. Corporate salaries are listed for six employees, as shown below. How much higher is the mean salary than the mode salary?

    $32,000 $36,000 $36,000
    $45,000 $51,000 $64,000

    (Average) (Skill 9.4)

    A. $8,000

    B. $9,000

    C. $12,000

    D. $15,000

38. A jar contains 3 red marbles, 5 white marbles, 1 green marble, and 15 blue marbles. If one marble is picked at random from the jar, what is the probability that it will be red?
    (Easy) (Skill 9.5)

    A. $\frac{1}{3}$

    B. $\frac{1}{8}$

    C. $\frac{3}{8}$

    D. $\frac{1}{24}$

39. A box contains 10 marbles, each of which is assigned a different number from 1 to 10. Linda will randomly draw two consecutive marbles. What is the probability that she will draw the marble numbered 1 on the first draw and any even-numbered marble on the second draw?
    (Rigorous) (Skill 9.5)

    A. 1/2

    B. 1/5

    C. 1/15

    D. 1/18

40. A sack of candy has 3 peppermints, 2 butterscotch drops, and 3 cinnamon drops. One candy is drawn and replaced, then another candy is drawn. What is the probability that both will be butterscotch?
    (Rigorous) (Skill 9.5)

    A. 1/2

    B. 1/28

    C. 1/4

    D. 1/16

41. -3 + 7 = -4   6(-10) = -60
    -5(-15) = 75   -3 + -8 = 11
    8 – 12 = -4   7 – -8 = 15

    Which best describes the type of error observed above?
    (Easy) (Skill 5.2)

    A. The student is incorrectly multiplying integers

    B. The student has incorrectly applied rules for adding integers to subtracting integers

    C. The student has incorrectly applied rules for multiplying integers to adding integers

    D. The student is incorrectly subtracting integers

42. **John is building a toy car with the same proportional dimensions as his real car, which is a Saturn. The tires of the Saturn are 18 inches in diameter and the steering wheel is 15 inches in diameter. If this toy car should have a steering wheel measuring 3/4 inch in diameter, what should be the diameter, in inches, of the tires of the toy car?**
    (Average) (Skill 6.3)

    A. 19/20

    B. 9/10

    C. 5/6

    D. 5/8

43. **Which of the following sets is closed under division?**
    (Average) (Skill 5.3)

    I) {½, 1, 2, 4}
    II) {-1, 1}
    III) {-1, 0, 1}

    A. I only

    B. II only

    C. III only

    D. I and II

44. **Evaluate $x^2 - 3x + 7$ when $x = 2$.**
    (Easy) (Skill 5.2)

    A. 7

    B. 5

    C. 3

    D. 9

45. **Suzanne flips an ordinary six-sided die once. What is the probability that the die shows face up the number 5 or 6?**
    (Easy) (Skill 9.6)

    A. 1/6

    B. 1/5

    C. 1/3

    D. 1/2

Answer Key: Mathematics Pretest

1.	A		24.	C
2.	B		25.	C
3.	C		26.	B
4.	C		27.	A
5.	A		28.	A
6.	A		29.	A
7.	A		30.	A
8.	B		31.	C
9.	B		32.	B
10.	C		33.	D
11.	A		34.	B
12.	A		35.	B
13.	C		36.	A
14.	B		37.	A
15.	D		38.	B
16.	D		39.	D
17.	D		40.	D
18.	D		41.	C
19.	C		42.	B
20.	B		43.	B
21.	C		44.	B
22.	C		45.	C
23.	B			

Rigor Table: Mathematics Pretest

	Easy 25%	Average 36%	Rigorous 34%
Questions	1, 4, 5, 18, 22, 23, 36, 38, 41, 44, 45	2, 3, 8, 10, 11, 13, 14, 19, 20, 24, 31, 32, 33, 34, 37, 42, 43	6, 7, 12, 15, 16, 17, 21, 25, 26, 27, 28, 29, 30, 35, 39, 40

Pretest with Rationales: Mathematics

1. Which of the following is correct?
   (Easy) (Skill 5.1)

   A.   2,365 > 2,340

   B.   0.75 > 1.25

   C.   3/4 < 1/16

   D.   -5 < -6

Answer: A. 2,365 > 2,340
2,365 is greater than 2,340. None of the other comparisons are correct.

2. Simplify:

   $$\frac{5^{-2} \times 5^3}{5^5 \times 5^{-7}}$$

   (Average) (Skill 5.3)

   A. 5^5

   B.   125

   C. $\frac{1}{125}$

   D.   25

Answer: B. 125

$$\frac{5^{-2} \times 5^3}{5^5 \times 5^{-7}} = \frac{5^{-2+3}}{5^{5-7}} = \frac{5}{5^{-2}} = 5^{1+2} = 5^3 = 125.$$

3. Choose the set in which the members are *not* equivalent.
   (Average) (Skill 5.1)

   A. 1/2, 0.5, 50%

   B. 10/5, 2.0, 200%

   C. 3/8, 0.385, 38.5%

   D. 7/10, 0.7, 70%

Answer: C. 3/8, 0.385, 38.5%
3/8 is equivalent to .375 and 37.5%.

4. The digit 8 in the number 975.086 is in the:
   (Easy) (Skill 5.1)

   A. Tenths place

   B. Ones place

   C. Hundredths place

   D. Hundreds place

Answer: C. Hundredths place
The digit 8 is in the hundredths place; the digit 0 is in the tenths place.

5. **The relations given below demonstrate the following addition and multiplication property of real numbers:**
   a + b = b + a
   ab = ba
   (Easy) (Skill 5.3)

   A. Commutative

   B. Associative

   C. Identity

   D. Inverse

Answer: A. Commutative
Both addition and multiplication of real numbers satisfy the commutative property according to which changing the order of the operands does not change the result of the operation.

6. **(3 x 9)^4 =**
   (Rigorous) (Skill 5.4)

   (3 x 9) (3 x 9) (27 x 27)
   (3 x 9) + (3 x 9)
   (12 x 36)
   (3 x 9) + (3 x 9) + (3 x 9) + (3 x 9)

Answer: A. (3 x 9) (3 x 9) (27 x 27)
(3 x 9)^4 = (3 x 9) (3 x 9) (3 x 9) (3 x 9), which, when solving two of the parentheses, is (3 x 9) (3 x 9) (27 x 27).

7. At a publishing company, Mona can proofread 300 pages in 5 hours while Lisa can proofread 360 pages in 4 hours. If they share the task of proofreading a 375-page document, how long will it take them to complete the job?
   (Rigorous) (Skill 5.2)

   A. 2.5 hours

   B. 5 hours

   C. 3 hours

   D. 3.5 hours

Answer: A. 2.5 hours
Since Mona proofreads 300/5 = 60 pages in one hour and Lisa proofreads 360/4 = 90 pages in one hour, together they can proofread 90 + 60 = 150 pages per hour. Hence, it would take then 375/150 = 2.5 hours to complete the job.

8. A student had 60 days to appeal the results of an exam. If the results were received on March 23, what was the last day that the student could appeal?
   (Average) (Skill 5.2)

   A. May 21

   B. May 22

   C. May 23

   D. May 24

Answer: B. May 22
Recall that there are 30 days in April and 31 in March. 8 days in March + 30 days in April + 22 days in May brings the student to a total of 60 days on May 22.

9. A coat is on sale for $135. If the discount offered is 25%, what was the original price of the coat?
   (Average) (Skill 5.2)

   A. $160

   B. $180

   C. $110

   D. $150

Answer: B. $180
Since the discount is 25%, the sale price $135 is 75% of the original price. Hence

$$\frac{135}{75} \times \frac{100}{1} = \frac{540}{3} = \$180$$

10. If three cups of concentrate are needed to make 2 gallons of fruit punch, how many cups are needed to make 5 gallons?
    (Average) (Skill 5.2)

    A.   6 cups

    B.   7 cups

    C.   7.5 cups

    D.   10 cups

Answer: C. 7.5 cups
Set up the proportion 3/2 = x/5, cross-multiply to obtain 15 = 2x, then divide both sides by 2.

11. A sofa sells for $520. If the retailer makes a 30% profit, what was the wholesale price?
    (Average) (Skill 5.2)

    A. $400

    B. $676

    C. $490

    D. $364

Answer: A. $400
Let x be the wholesale price; then $x + .30x = 520$, $1.30x = 520$. Divide both sides by 1.30.

12. Kendra needs to paint one rectangular wall of her bedroom, which measures 18 feet by 10 feet. Each container of paint she will use can cover 15 square feet and costs $9.98. What is the best approximation for the total cost of the paint she will need?
    (Rigorous) (Skill 6.5)

    A. $120

    B. $180

    C. $240

    D. $270

Answer: A. $120
The total number of square feet that Kendra needs to paint is $(18)(10) = 180$. Since each container of paint can cover 15 square feet, she will need $180 / 15 = 12$ containers. Each container costs $9.98, which rounds off to $10. Thus, the total cost of the paint is approximately $(12)(10) = \$120$.

13. Jason can run a distance of 50 yards in 6.5 seconds. At this rate, how many feet can he run in a time of 26 seconds?
    (Average) (Skill 6.4)

    A.   200

    B.   400

    C.   600

    D.   800

Answer: C. 600
26/6.5 = 4, so Jason can run a distance of (4)(50) = 200 yards in 26 seconds. Since 1 yard is equivalent to 3 feet, 200 yards is equivalent to (200)(3) = 600 feet.

14. Solve for x:

    $3(5 + 3x) - 8 = 88$

    (Average) (Skill 8.3)

    A.   30

    B.   9

    C.   4.5

    D.   27

Answer: B. 9
$3(5 + 3x) - 8 = 88$; $15 + 9x - 8 = 88$; $7 + 9x = 88$; $9x = 81$; $x = 9$.

15. Solve for *x*:

    | 2*x* + 3 | > 4

    (Rigorous) (Skill 8.3)

    A. $-\frac{7}{2} > x > \frac{1}{2}$

    B. $-\frac{1}{2} > x > \frac{7}{2}$

    C. $x < \frac{7}{2}$ or $x < -\frac{1}{2}$

    D. $x < -\frac{7}{2}$ or $x > \frac{1}{2}$

Answer: D. $x < -\frac{7}{2}$ or $x > \frac{1}{2}$

The quantity within the absolute value symbols must be either > 4 or < –4. Solve the two inequalities 2*x* + 3 > 4 or 2*x* + 3 < –4.

16. You are helping students list the steps needed to solve the word problem:

"Mr. Jones is 5 times as old as his son. Two years later he will be 4 times as old as his son. How old is Mr. Jones?"

One of the students makes the following list:

Assume Mr. Jones' son is x years old. Express Mr. Jones' age in terms of x.
Write how old they will be two years later in terms of x.
Solve the equation for x.
Multiply the answer by 5 to get Mr. Jones' age.

What step is missing between steps 2 and 3?
(Rigorous) (Skill 8.2)

A. Write an equation setting Mr. Jones' age equal to 5 times his son's age

B. Write an equation setting Mr. Jones' age two years later equal to 5 times his son's age two years later

C. Write an equation setting Mr. Jones' age equal to 4 times his son's age

D. Write an equation setting Mr. Jones' age two years later equal to 4 times his son's age two years later

Answer: D. Write an equation setting Mr. Jones' age two years later equal to 4 times his son's age two years later

For step 2, we can represent Mr. Jones' age in two years as $5x + 2$ and his son's age in two years as $x + 2$. But before we can solve an equation for x, we need to state that Mr. Jones' age in two years will be 4 times his son's age in two years. This will show the relationship between father and son in two years. The actual equation becomes $5x + 2 = 4(x + 2)$, which will lead to $x = 6$ (the son's current age). Note that Mr. Jones' current age must be $(5)(6) = 30$. As a check, we observe that in two years the son will be 8 years old and Mr. Jones will be 32 years old.

17. Which of the following points does *not* lie on the graph of $|y + 3| < |x - 3|$?

(Rigorous) (Skill 8.2)

  A. (-5, 4)

  B. (-6, 0)

  C. (-3, -4)

  D. (7, 7)

Answer: D. (7, 7)
By substitution, we get $|7 + 3| < |7 + 3|$ ⊗ $|10| < |4|$ ⊗ $10 < 4$, which is false. Thus, (7, 7) does not lie on the graph of $|y + 3| < |x - 3|$. Note that by substituting the three points listed in the other answer choices, the inequality is correct. For Option A, we get $|7| < |-8|$, which is true. For Option B, we get $|3| < |-9|$, which is true. For Option C, we get $|-1| < |-6|$, which is true.

18. What is the next term in the following sequence?

{0.005, 0.03, 0.18, 1.08…}

(Easy) (Skill 8.1)

  A. 1.96

  B. 2.16

  C. 3.32

  D. 6.48

Answer: D. 6.48
This is a geometric sequence where each term is obtained by multiplying the preceding term by the common ratio 6. Thus, the next term in the sequence is 1.08 x 6 = 6.48.

19. {1,4,7,10, . . .}
    What is the 40th term in this sequence?
    (Average) (Skill 8.1)

    A.   43

    B.   121

    C.   118

    D.   120

Answer: C. 118
This is an arithmetic sequence with first term 1 and common difference 3. Hence, the 40th term is 1 + (40 − 1)3 = 1 + 39 x 3 = 1 + 117 = 118.

20. **What is the *x*-intercept of the line represented by 4*x* + 2*y* = 12?**
    (Rigorous) (Skill 8.3)

    A.   (0, 6)

    B.   (3, 0)

    C.   (0, 3)

    D.   (0, 8)

Answer: B. (3, 0)
Let *y* = 0 and solve for *x:*
4*x* + 2(0) = 12
4*x* + 0 = 12
4*x* = 12
x = 3
(3, 0) is the *x*-intercept.

21. A student has taken three tests in his algebra class for which the mean score is 88. He will take one more test and his final grade will be the mean of all four tests. He wants to achieve a final grade of 90. Which one of the following is the correct procedure to determine the score he needs on the fourth test?
(Rigorous) (Skill 8.2)

    A.   He needs a score 92 since (88 + 92) / 2 = 90.

    B.   He needs a score of 89.5 since (88 + 90 + 90 + 90) / 4 = 89.5.

    C.   He needs a score of 96 since (88 + 88 + 88 + 96) / 4 = 90.

    D.   He cannot achieve a final grade of 90 since each of his scores on the first three tests is less than 90.

Answer: C. He needs a score of 96 since (88 + 88 + 88 + 96) / 4 = 90.
The sum of all four tests must be (90)(4) = 360 in order to achieve a mean score of 90. Since he has averaged 88 on his first three tests, the sum of his scores thus far is (88)(3) = 264. Therefore he needs a score of 360 − 264 = 96 on his fourth test.

22. Which of the following shapes is *not* a parallelogram?
    (Easy) (Skill 7.1)

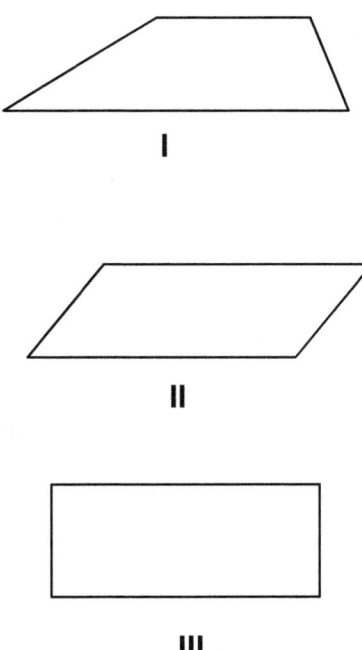

I

II

III

A. I and III

B. II and III

C. I only

D. I, II, and III

Answer: C. I
A parallelogram is a quadrilateral with two pairs of parallel sides.

23. An isosceles triangle has:
    (Easy) (Skill 7.1)

    A.   Three equal sides

    B.   Two equal sides

    C.   No equal sides

    D.   Two equal sides in some cases, no equal sides in others

Answer: B. Two equal sides

24. Given similar polygons with corresponding sides of lengths 9 and 15, find the perimeter of the smaller polygon if the perimeter of the larger polygon is 150 units.
    (Average) (Skill 7.2)

    A.   54

    B.   135

    C.   90

    D.   126

Answer: C. 90
The perimeters of similar polygons are directly proportional to the lengths of their sides, therefore 9/15 = x/150. Cross-multiply to obtain 1350 = 15x, then divide by 15 to obtain the perimeter of the smaller polygon.

25. Ginny and Nick head back to their respective colleges after being home for the weekend. They leave their house at the same time and drive for 4 hours. Ginny drives due south at the average rate of 60 miles per hour, and Nick drives due east at the average rate of 60 miles per hour. What is the straight-line distance between them, in miles, at the end of the 4 hours?
(Rigorous) (Skill 7.2)

A. $120\sqrt{2}$

B. 240

C. $240\sqrt{2}$

D. 288

Answer: C. $240\sqrt{2}$
Draw a picture.

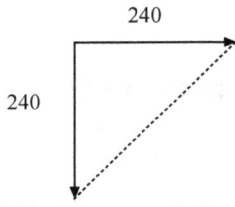

We have a right triangle, so we can use the Pythagorean theorem to find the distance between the two points.

$240^2 + 240^2 = c^2$

$2(240)^2 = c^2$

$240\sqrt{2} = c$

26. Given segment *AC* with *B* as its midpoint, find the coordinates of *C* if *A* = (5, 7) and *B* = (3, 6.5).
    (Rigorous) (Skill 7.3)

    A. (4, 6.5)

    B. (1, 6)

    C. (2, 0.5)

    D. (16, 1)

Answer: B. (1, 6)
Let (x,y) be the coordinates of *C*. Using the midpoint formula, the coordinates of *B* can be expressed as follows:

$3 = (5+x)/2$; $6.5 = (7 + y)/2$

Solving for *x* and *y*, we get $x = 1$ and $y = 6$.

27. Which one of the following sets of points on a coordinate plane defines an isosceles right triangle?
    (Rigorous) (Skill 7.3)

    A. (4,0), (0,4), (4,4)

    B. (4,0), (0,6), (4,4)

    C. (0,0), (0,4), (5,2)

    D. (0,0), (5,0), (5,2)

Answer: A. (4,0), (0,4), (4,4)
Option D defines a right triangle that is not isosceles, Option C defines an isosceles triangle that is not right, and Option B defines a triangle that is neither isosceles nor right.

28. The speed of light in space is about 3×10^8 meters per second. Express this in Kilometers per hour.
   (Rigorous) (Skill 6.2)

   A. 1.08×10^9 Km/hr

   B. 3.0×10^{11} Km/hr

   C. 1.08×10^{12} Km/hr

   D. 1.08×10^{15} Km/hr

Answer: A. 1.08×10^9 Km/hr

$$3 \times 10^8 \frac{m}{s} = 3 \times 10^8 \frac{m}{s} \times \frac{1 Km}{1000 m} \times \frac{3600 s}{1 hr} = 108 \times 10^7 \frac{Km}{hr} = 1.08 \times 10^9 \frac{Km}{hr}$$

29. Given a 30-meter x 60-meter garden with a circular fountain with a 5-meter radius, calculate the area of the portion of the garden *not* occupied by the fountain.
   (Rigorous) (Skill 6.1)

   A.   1,721 m²

   B.   1,879 m²

   C.   2,585 m²

   D.   1,015 m²

Answer: A. 1,721 m²
Find the area of the garden and then subtract the area of the fountain: 30(60) − $\pi(5)^2$, or approximately 1,721 square meters.

30. What is the length of a fourth of the circumference of a circle with a diameter of 24 cm?
(Rigorous) (Skill 6.1)

    A.   18.85

    B.   75.4

    C.   32.45

    D.   20.75

Answer: A. 18.85
The circumference of the circle is πd, where d is 24. π(24)= 75.4; a fourth of that is 18.85.

31. What percentage of students got a C grade?
(Average) (Skill 9.1)

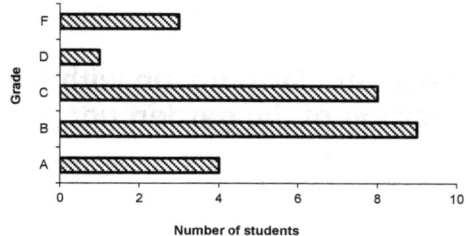

    A.   35

    B.   8

    C.   32

    D.   40

Answer: C. 32
The total number of students = 4 + 9 + 8 + 1 + 3 = 25. The number of students who got C = 8. Hence, the percentage of students that got C = (8/25) x 100= 32.

32. If George spends $300 per month on his utilities, how much does he spend during a two-month period for the combined total of his mortgage, food, and miscellaneous items?
(Average) (Skill 9.1)

    A. $2,400

    B. $1,800

    C. $1,200

    D. $900

Answer: B. $1,800
Since George's utilities represent 25% of the entire budget, his total expenditures for all four items per month equal $300 / 25% = $1,200. This means that the amount he spends per month on mortgage, food, and miscellaneous items is $1,200 − $300 = $900. Finally, the total amount spent for the mortgage, food, and miscellaneous items for a two-month period is ($900)(2) = $1,800.

33. You are creating a pie chart to show the expenses for a business. If employee pay is 40% of the total expenditure, what central angle will you use to show that segment of the pie chart?
   (Average) (Skill 9.1)

   A. 72°

   B. 80°

   C. 40°

   D. 144°

Answer: D. 144°
Since employee pay is 40% of the total, the central angle will be 40% of 360° = (40/100) x 360° = 144°.

34. Which of the following is the most accurate inference that can be made from the graph shown below?
(Average) (Skill 9.1)

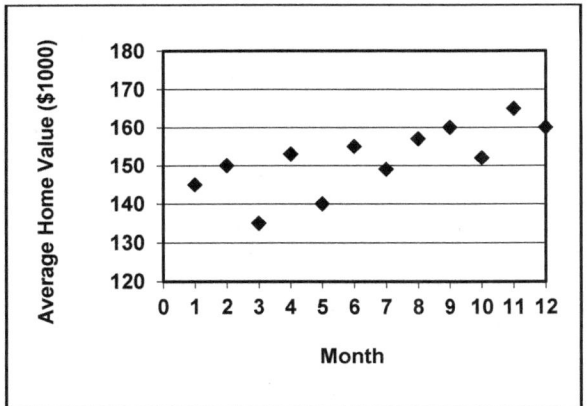

- A. The average home value shows a decreasing trend over the 12-month period

- B. The average home value shows an increasing trend over the 12-month period

- C. The average home value stays about the same over the 12-month period

- D. The data fluctuates too much to make any comment about the trend

Answer: B. The average home value shows an increasing trend over the 12-month period
Even though the data fluctuates, it shows an unmistakable upward trend toward the right.

35. Melissa scores 60, 68, and 75 in the first three of five tests. What should her average score be for the last two tests so that her mean test score for the five tests is 70?
   (Rigorous) (Skill 9.3)

   A.   70

   B.   73.5

   C.   75.5

   D.   85

Answer: B. 73.5
Let Melissa's average score for the last two tests be x. Then,
$60 + 68 + 75 + 2x = 70 \times 5$
$2x = 350 - 203 = 147$
$x = 73.5$.

36. Find the median of the following set of data: 14 3 7 6 11 20
    (Easy) (Skill 9.3)

   A.   9

   B.   8.5

   C.   7

   D.   11

Answer: A. 9
Place the numbers in ascending order: 3 6 7 11 14 20. Find the average of the middle two numbers $(7 + 11)/2 = 9$.

37. Corporate salaries are listed for six employees, as shown below. How much higher is the mean salary than the mode salary?

$32,000 $36,000 $36,000
$45,000 $51,000 $64,000

(Average) (Skill 9.4)

A. $8,000

B. $9,000

C. $12,000

D. $15,000

Answer: A. $8,000
The mean salary is ($32,000 + $36,000 + $36,000 + $45,000 + $51,000 + $64,000)/6 = $264,000/6 = $44,000. The mode salary is $36,000 because it appears more often than any of the other salaries. Thus, the mean salary is $44,000 − $36,000 = $8,000 higher than the mode salary.

38. A jar contains 3 red marbles, 5 white marbles, 1 green marble, and 15 blue marbles. If one marble is picked at random from the jar, what is the probability that it will be red?
(Easy) (Skill 9.5)

A. $\dfrac{1}{3}$

B. $\dfrac{1}{8}$

C. $\dfrac{3}{8}$

D. $\dfrac{1}{24}$

Answer: B. $\dfrac{1}{8}$
The total number of marbles is 24 and the number of red marbles is 3. Thus, the probability of picking a red marble from the jar is 3/24=1/8.

39. A box contains 10 marbles, each of which is assigned a different number from 1 to 10. Linda will randomly draw two consecutive marbles. What is the probability that she will draw the marble numbered 1 on the first draw and any even-numbered marble on the second draw? *(Rigorous) (Skill 9.5)*

   A.   1/2

   B.   1/5

   C.   1/15

   D.   1/18

Answer: D. 1/18
For the first draw, there is only the one marble numbered 1 out of 10 marbles, so the associated probability for drawing this marble is 1/10. For the second draw, there is no replacement of the first drawn marble, so there are only nine marbles left. There are five even-numbered marbles, namely, the ones numbered 2, 4, 6, 8, and 10. The probability of drawing an even-numbered marble becomes 5/9. Therefore, the required probability for this problem is (1/10)(5/9) = 5/90, which reduces to 1/18.

40. A sack of candy has 3 peppermints, 2 butterscotch drops, and 3 cinnamon drops. One candy is drawn and replaced, then another candy is drawn. What is the probability that both will be butterscotch? *(Rigorous) (Skill 9.5)*

   A.   1/2

   B.   1/28

   C.   1/4

   D.   1/16

Answer: D. 1/16
With replacement, the probability of obtaining a butterscotch on the first draw is 2/8 and the probability of drawing a butterscotch on the second draw is also 2/8. Multiply and reduce to lowest terms.

41. -3 + 7 = -4   6(-10) = -60
    -5(-15) = 75   -3 + -8 = 11
    8 – 12 = -4   7 – -8 = 15

   Which best describes the type of error observed above?
   (Easy) (Skill 5.2)

   A.   The student is incorrectly multiplying integers.

   B.   The student has incorrectly applied rules for adding integers to subtracting integers.

   C.   The student has incorrectly applied rules for multiplying integers to adding integers.

   D.   The student is incorrectly subtracting integers.

Answer: C. The student has incorrectly applied rules for multiplying integers to adding integers.
The errors are in the following: -3 + 7= -4 and –3 + -8 = 11, where the student seems to be using the rules for signs when multiplying, instead of the rules for signs when adding.

42. **John is building a toy car with the same proportional dimensions as his real car, which is a Saturn. The tires of the Saturn are 18 inches in diameter and the steering wheel is 15 inches in diameter. If this toy car should have a steering wheel measuring 3/4 inch in diameter, what should be the diameter, in inches, of the tires of the toy car?**
   (Average) (Skill 6.3)

   A.   19/20

   B.   9/10

   C.   5/6

   D.   5/8

Answer: B. 9/10
The ratio of the size of the steering wheel on the Saturn to the steering wheel on the toy car is (15)/(3/4), which simplifies to 20/1. This means that since the diameter of the tires on the Saturn measure 18 inches, the diameter of the tires on the toy car should be (1/20)(18) = 9/10 inch.

43. Which of the following sets is closed under division?
(Average) (Skill 5.3)

I) {½, 1, 2, 4}
II) {-1, 1}
III) {-1, 0, 1}

   A.   I only

   B.   II only

   C.   III only

   D.   I and II

Answer: B. II only

I is not closed because $\frac{4}{.5} = 8$ and 8 is not in the set. III is not closed because $\frac{1}{0}$ is undefined. II is closed because $\frac{-1}{1} = -1, \frac{1}{-1} = -1, \frac{1}{1} = 1, \frac{-1}{-1} = 1$ and all the answers are in the set.

44. Evaluate $x^2 - 3x + 7$ when $x = 2$.
(Easy) (Skill 5.2)

   A.   7

   B.   5

   C.   3

   D.   9

Answer: B. 5

Substitute $x = 2$ in the expression to get $2^2 - 3 \times 2 + 7 = 4 - 6 + 7 = 5$.

45. Suzanne flips an ordinary six-sided die once. What is the probability that the die shows face up the number 5 or 6?
(Easy) (Skill 9.6)

    A.   1/6

    B.   1/5

    C.   1/3

    D.   1/2

Answer: C. 1/3
There are two successful outcomes, namely, the number 5 or the number 6, out of a total of six possible outcomes. Thus, the associated probability is 2/6 = 1/3.

Reading Pretest

DIRECTIONS: Read the following passage and answer the questions that follow.

The Eiffel Tower in Paris, France, is probably the country's most recognizable symbol. Not only is the tower an obvious symbol, but it is also an incredible work of art that was designed by Gustave Eiffel. The tower, which was opened March 31, 1889, was originally built for the Universal Exhibition and was only meant to stand for twenty years then be destroyed. Luckily, the tower still stands to this day in the original post it was constructed.

   Between 1889 when the tower opened and December 31, 2008, 243,376,000 people have visited the 324-meter iron tower. In order to ride to the second floor of the tower, a visitor must pay 8 francs to ride the elevator. To ride all the way to the top floor, a visitor must pay 13 francs. For only 4.50 francs, a visitor can take the stairs. Unfortunately, guests must climb 115 meters to reach the second floor, and stairs are not available for visitors who wish to go to the top of the tower. In other words, visitors who wish to go all the way to the top of the tower must take the elevator.

1. **What is the main idea of the passage?**
   (Average) (Skill 10.1)

   A. The Eiffel Tower opened on March 31, 1889

   B. Many people have visited the Eiffel Tower since it opened

   C. Visitors can take the elevator or the stairs to reach the top of the tower

   D. The Eiffel Tower is a well-known symbol around the world

2. **Why did the author write this article?**
   (Average) (Skill 11.1)

   A. To entertain

   B. To persuade

   C. To describe

   D. To inform

3. **What is the best summary of the second paragraph?**
   (Rigorous) (Skill 10.2)

   A. Visitors can ride an elevator or take the stairs to reach certain heights of the Eiffel Tower

   B. The Eiffel Tower is very tall and stands 324 meters high

   C. The elevator at the Eiffel Tower only reaches 115 meters

   D. Visitors must pay in order to climb to the top of the Eiffel Tower

4. **How is the passage organized?** *(Average) (Skill 11.2)*

   A. Cause and effect

   B. Compare and contrast

   C. Statement support

   D. Sequence of events

5. **What comparison is made in the first paragraph?** *(Rigorous) (Skill 11.6)*

   A. The Eiffel Tower is in Paris, France but is enjoyed by the world

   B. The Eiffel Tower opened in 1889 and is still in the same spot today

   C. The Eiffel Tower is recognizable and it serves as a country's symbol

   D. The Eiffel Tower is a great symbol of France and a work of art

6. **By using the word "luckily" in the final sentence of the first paragraph, what is the author implying?** *(Rigorous) (Skill 10.1)*

   A. That tearing the tower down as originally intended would have been a bad decision

   B. It is a good thing for France that the tower remains in the same spot it was built

   C. If the tower had been torn down, Gustave, its designer would have been angry

   D. The Universal Exhibition can now take place in the exact same spot someday since the tower remains

7. **What words does the author use in paragraph 2 to clarify information for the reader?**
(Average) (Skill 11.6)

   A. Between

   B. In order to

   C. Unfortunately

   D. In other words

8. **What would have been the best transition word for the author to use to connect these two sentences?**
(Easy) (Skill 10.1)

   In order to ride to the second floor of the tower, a visitor must pay 8 francs to ride the elevator. To ride all the way to the top floor, a visitor must pay 13 francs.

   A. Next,

   B. Beyond,

   C. For example,

   D. Consequently,

9. **What does the word "pang" mean in the sentence below?**
(Easy) (Skill 10.3)

   Standing outside her homeroom, Lauren watched other children enter the room and overheard them sharing stories about their summer adventures. She couldn't help but feel a pang of loneliness as she thought of her best friend Morgan back in Colorado.

   A. Pain

   B. Hint

   C. Depression

   D. Song

10. **What does the word "convoluted" mean in the sentence below?**
(Easy) (Skill 10.3)

    Misty listened to Marty intently. But as Marty revealed more of her plan, Misty wasn't sure she wanted anything to do with it. Marty's plan was convoluted and twisted and, quite frankly, Misty was worried about her own safety.

    A. Strange

    B. Straight

    C. Thorough

    D. Polluted

11. The book *The Giver* by Lois Lowry is a great book. The characters are interesting and they are unique. Everyone who reads *The Giver* will enjoy it and not be able to put it down.

    Is this a valid or invalid argument?
    (Average) (Skill 11.7)

    A. Valid

    B. Invalid

12. I-95 is the best route to take from Virginia to Washington, DC. There are many rest stops along the way so it is easy to stop and get gas, food, and use the restrooms when necessary. There is also an HOV lane that allows those traveling with others to bypass single traveler cars.

    Is this a valid or invalid argument?
    (Average) (Skill 11.7)

    A. Valid

    B. Invalid

DIRECTIONS: Read the following passage and answer the questions that follow.

This writer has often been asked to tutor hospitalized children with cystic fibrosis. While undergoing all the precautionary measures to see these children (for example, scrubbing thoroughly and donning a face mask and sterile gown), she has wondered why parents subject these children to the pressures of schooling and trying to catch up on what they have missed because of hospitalization, which is a normal part of cystic fibrosis patients' lives. These children undergo so many tortuous treatments a day that it seems cruel to expect them to learn as normal children do, especially when their life expectancies are so short.

13. What type of organizational pattern does the author use?
    (Rigorous) (Skill 11.2)

    A. Classification

    B. Example, clarification, and definition

    C. Comparison and contrast

    D. Cause and effect

14. Is there evidence of bias in this paragraph?
    (Rigorous) (Skill 11.3)

    A. Yes

    B. No

15. Elementary school is better than middle school.

    Is this sentence a fact or an opinion?
    (Easy) (Skill 11.3)

    A. Fact

    B. Opinion

16. Letter grades are given at Thomas Jefferson Middle School.

    Is this sentence a fact or an opinion?
    (Easy) (Skill 11.3)

    A. Fact

    B. Opinion

17. The science fair will take place at 4:00 on Saturday, March 13.

    Is this sentence a fact or an opinion?
    (Easy) (Skill 11.3)

    A. Fact

    B. Opinion

18. The science fair will be a lot of fun so everyone should attend.

    Is this sentence a fact or an opinion?
    (Easy) (Skill 11.3)

    A. Fact

    B. Opinion

19. *Thank you so much for the gift you sent for my birthday. It was nice of you to send me a gift and remember that my birthday was last week. Your generosity is appreciated. Thanks again.*
    John

    What conclusion can be drawn from the above letter?
    (Rigorous) (Skill 11.8)

    A. The author and the gift giver are related

    B. The author is a child who received a gift

    C. The gift was a toy and the author liked it

    D. The author didn't really like the gift

20. *Even after I turned the lock correctly it still wouldn't open. My combination is 32-41-12; I hope this will help you get to the bottom of the problem. All of my school supplies are locked inside, and I must have them in order to be successful in my classes.*

    What conclusion can be drawn from the paragraph above? *(Average) (Skill 11.8)*

    A. A teacher's belongings are locked inside of her car

    B. A student is having trouble with his locker

    C. A student's gym locker is jammed

    D. A traveler's locker is jammed

DIRECTIONS: Read the following passage and answer the questions that follow.

It is not news to anyone who has been following the changes in the economy that people are spending less. This is a wise decision by all consumers and since people are reevaluating their spending, it is necessary for companies to reevaluate their plans for growth. Many companies that were spending money on security have had to shift their focus elsewhere. A number of companies have made the decision to focus on virtualization—when one computer completes the jobs of many. Instead of a lot of computers doing a lot of jobs, one central, or main computer, will control all of the smaller jobs.

  Due to the recession, companies are fighting for every little bit of business they can grab. Therefore, in today's rat race every little change might make a big difference. Companies believe that using one computer will save them money because one large computer can do more than one task at a time. Actually, it is considered the human version of multitasking. Furthermore, by moving toward virtualization, businesses can save energy. Businesses can reduce the number of computers, thus reducing the amount of energy that they use as a business, and saving additional time. With fewer machines there is less maintenance and time spent on maintenance can be spent elsewhere. With competition at an all-time high, small changes can make a big difference and virtualization meets this challenge that now faces the modern day business model. Only time will tell if the small change will have a big effect.

21. **How does the author feel about virtualization?**
    (Rigorous) (Skill 11.5)

    A. The author thinks that it is a great idea

    B. The author feels that it is the only way to handle the recession

    C. The author isn't convinced that the small change will have a big effect

    D. The author believes it should have been introduced a long time ago

22. **How does the author feel about today's business environment?**
    (Rigorous) (Skill 11.5)

    A. The author believes that it is difficult to succeed in today's business environment

    B. The author thinks that businesses have gotten too big

    C. The author feels that only people are capable of multitasking

    D. The author thinks that businesses rely too heavily on machines to do a human's work

23. **From this passage, one can infer that:**
 (Rigorous) (Skill 11.8)

 A. The economy is doing well and companies are spending their money wisely

 B. The economy used to be doing better and consumers, as well as companies, have had to make adjustments

 C. The stock market is what drives consumer confidence and company sales

 D. Many companies do whatever other companies are doing

24. **From this passage, one can infer that:**
 (Rigorous) (Skill 11.8)

 A. Before the economy was doing poorly, companies focused their spending in other areas

 B. Company workers are finding other jobs because of the bad economy

 C. Employees will lose their jobs due to the recession

 D. Companies are trying virtualization instead of resorting to employee layoffs to save money

DIRECTIONS: Read the following passage and answer the questions that follow.

Megan was about to plant the last plant in the sunniest spot in the yard. She worked the soft, pliable soil to steady the plant around the roots. She filled in the empty area around the roots with more dirt. Recently, Megan had decided that she was going to plant a butterfly garden in her yard. She had worked very hard over the past week to clear the area so she would be able to plant this week while her grandparents were visiting. She and her grandmother had just returned from the nursery where they bought some petunias, peonies, and hollyhocks. Consequently, these plants would attract all sorts of butterflies.

25. **What is the main idea of the passage?**
 (Average) (Skill 10.1)

 A. How to create a butterfly garden

 B. Megan was in the final stages of creating her butterfly garden

 C. Petunias, peonies, and hollyhocks need to be planted in a sunny spot

 D. A butterfly garden is the name for a garden that contains peonies

26. **Why did the author write this article?**
    (Average) (Skill 11.1)

    A. To convince the reader to plant a butterfly garden

    B. To teach the reader how to plant a butterfly garden

    C. To encourage the reader to spend time with their family

    D. To amuse the reader with a story about planting a garden

27. **How is the passage organized?**
    (Average) (Skill 11.2)

    A. Sequence of events

    B. Cause and effect

    C. Statement support

    D. Compare and contrast

28. **What cause and effect relationship exists in this paragraph?**
    (Rigorous) (Skill 11.6)

    A. Because it is sunny, the butterflies will visit Megan's garden

    B. Because Megan worked so hard this week, her grandparents came to visit

    C. Because Megan planted certain plants, butterflies will like her garden

    D. Because it was sunny, Megan was planting her last plant

29. **By using the word "consequently" in the final sentence of the first paragraph, what is the author implying?**
    (Rigorous) (Skill 10.1)

    A. That Megan did not want butterflies to visit her garden

    B. Megan's grandmother did not want butterflies to visit the garden

    C. There would be consequences if the butterflies came to the garden

    D. The plants were purchased so that butterflies would visit the garden

30. **What transition word could the author have used to connect these two sentences?** *(Average) (Skill 10.1)*

    She worked with the soft, pliable soil to steady the plant around the roots. She filled in the empty area around the roots with more dirt.

    A. Third,

    B. Hence,

    C. Next,

    D. Prior to that,

31. **What does the word "pliable" mean in the second sentence?** *(Average) (Skill 10.3)*

    A. Wet

    B. Organic

    C. Bendable

    D. Sandy

DIRECTIONS: Read the following passage and answer the questions that follow.

The Fog and *The Hitchhiker* are both suspenseful. Both plays also contain ghost characters. Ghosts frighten me. *The Fog* has three ghost characters named Eben, Zeke, and a wounded man. The reader does not realize that these men are ghosts however, until the end of the play. In *The Hitchhiker*, there is one ghost character known as "The Gray Man" who stalks the main character, Ronald Adams, until the end of the play. It is not revealed however, who the hitchhiker is until the end. The reader needs to make their own decision about his significance. The Gray Man is a little creepy.

The Fog takes place in Gettysburg, Pennsylvania during a war. *The Hitchhiker* on the other hand, is a more modern play and takes place during the 1930s and 1940s as a traveler drives to many cities across the country.

32. **How is the passage organized?** *(Average) (Skill 11.2)*

    A. Compare and contrast

    B. Cause and effect

    C. Sequence of events

    D. Statement support

33. **Which sentence in the passage is irrelevant?**
    (Average) (Skill 11.6)

    A. *The Fog* and *The Hitchhiker* are both suspenseful.

    B. Both plays also contain ghost characters.

    C. Ghosts frighten me.

    D. *The Fog* has three ghost characters named Eben, Zeke, and a wounded man.

34. **Which sentence in the passage is irrelevant?**
    (Rigorous) (Skill 11.6)

    A. The reader does not realize that these men are ghosts.

    B. In *The Hitchhiker* there is one ghost character known as "The Gray Man."

    C. It is not revealed who the hitchhiker is until the end of the play.

    D. The Gray Man is a little creepy.

DIRECTIONS: Read the following passage and answer the questions that follow.

Smells were coming from the kitchen that repelled Kim further and further away. But he couldn't get far away enough to escape the odor. His sister Lee was experimenting with a new recipe. Lee often cooked new exotic and foreign dishes. Sometimes this was great for Kim because he was always the first one to try one of Lee's newest creations. He remembered the time that she made zesty fruit salsa with cinnamon pita chips. Maybe he could request that she make that again instead of what she was cooking now.

35. **What conclusion can be drawn from the passage?**
    (Rigorous) (Skill 11.8)

    A. Kim is a good cook

    B. Lee enjoys cooking

    C. Kim doesn't enjoy Lee's cooking

    D. Lee only makes desserts

36. **What can be inferred about Kim and Lee's relationship from the passage?**
    (Rigorous) (Skill 11.8)

    A. Overall, Kim and Lee get along

    B. Kim and Lee do not get along well

    C. Kim only tells Lee about dishes he doesn't like

    D. Kim and Lee only share an interest in cooking

DIRECTIONS: Read the following passage and answer the questions that follow.

Have you ever heard the expression, "Busy as a bee"? Well, nothing could be truer. Bees are very busy insects, and they are very interesting. Bees live in colonies where each member has a specific job. In honeybee colonies, there are queens, drones, and workers. The queen is the largest bee and lays all the eggs. The drones do not have stingers, and their job is to mate with the queen. Most of the bees in the colony are workers. They care for the queen, remove trash, build the nest, guard the entrance, and collect nectar, pollen, and water. Sounds like most worker bees are males. The bees that go out to collect are called foragers.

37. **What is the main idea of the passage?**
    (Average) (Skill 10.1)

    A. Bees live in colonies

    B. There are three different types of bees

    C. Each type of bee has a specific job that is important to the colonies' survival

    D Foragers are also known as collectors and they have an important job

38. **What does the word "forage" mean?**
    (Easy) (Skill 10.3)

    A. Work hard

    B. To be busy

    C. To care for

    D. Go and collect

39. **Which is an opinion contained in this passage?**
    (Average) (Skill 11.3)

    A. Bees are very interesting

    B. Bees live in colonies

    C. Each colony has a queen

    D. The queen is the largest bee

40. **From this passage you can see that the author thinks:**
    (Rigorous) (Skill 11.5)

    A. Bees lay large eggs

    B. Drones have the best job

    C. Male bees work very hard

    D. Foragers have the most important job

Answer Key: Reading Pretest

1. D
2. D
3. A
4. C
5. D
6. A
7. D
8. D
9. B
10. A
11. B
12. A
13. B
14. A
15. B
16. A
17. A
18. B
19. D
20. B
21. C
22. A
23. B
24. A
25. B
26. D
27. A
28. C
29. D
30. C
31. C
32. A
33. C
34. D
35. B
36. A
37. C
38. D
39. A
40. C

Rigor Table: Reading Pretest

	Easy 20%	Average 40%	Rigorous 40%
Questions	8, 9, 10, 15, 16, 17, 18, 38	1, 2, 4, 7, 11, 13, 20, 25, 26, 27, 30, 31, 32, 33, 37, 39	3, 5, 6, 12, 14, 19, 21, 22, 23, 24, 28, 29, 34, 35, 36, 40

Pretest with Rationales: Reading

DIRECTIONS: Read the following passage and answer the questions that follow.

The Eiffel Tower in Paris, France, is probably the country's most recognizable symbol. Not only is the tower an obvious symbol, but it is also an incredible work of art that was designed by Gustave Eiffel. The tower, which was opened March 31, 1889, was originally built for the Universal Exhibition and was only meant to stand for twenty years then be destroyed. Luckily, the tower still stands to this day in the original post it was constructed.

Between 1889 when the tower opened and December 31, 2008, 243,376,000 people have visited the 324-meter iron tower. In order to ride to the second floor of the tower, a visitor must pay 8 francs to ride the elevator. To ride all the way to the top floor, a visitor must pay 13 francs. For only 4.50 francs, a visitor can take the stairs. Unfortunately, guests must climb 115 meters to reach the second floor, and stairs are not available for visitors who wish to go to the top of the tower. In other words, visitors who wish to go all the way to the top of the tower must take the elevator.

1. **What is the main idea of the passage?**
   (Average) (Skill 10.1)

   A. The Eiffel Tower opened on March 31, 1889

   B. Many people have visited the Eiffel Tower since it opened

   C. Visitors can take the elevator or the stairs to reach the top of the tower

   D. The Eiffel Tower is a well-known symbol around the world

Answer: D. The Eiffel Tower is a well-known symbol around the world
Options A, B, and C are all details that are very specific and support the main idea that the Eiffel Tower is a well-known symbol around the world.

2. **Why did the author write this article?**
   (Average) (Skill 11.1)

   A. To entertain

   B. To persuade

   C. To describe

   D. To inform

Answer: D. To inform
The author wrote this article to teach its readers about the Eiffel Tower—in other words, to inform them.

3. **What is the best summary of the second paragraph?**
   (Rigorous) (Skill 10.2)

   A. Visitors can ride an elevator or take the stairs to reach certain heights of the Eiffel Tower

   B. The Eiffel Tower is very tall and stands 324 meters high

   C. The elevator at the Eiffel Tower only reaches 115 meters

   D. Visitors must pay in order to climb to the top of the Eiffel Tower

Answer: A. Visitors can ride an elevator or take the stairs to reach certain heights of the Eiffel Tower
Options B, C, and D are all details that support the main idea of the second paragraph.

4. **How is the passage organized?**
   (Average) (Skill 11.2)

   A. Cause and effect

   B. Compare and contrast

   C. Statement support

   D. Sequence of events

Answer: C. Statement support
The main idea of each paragraph is stated and then supporting sentences follow. Therefore, this is a "statement support" organization example.

5. **What comparison is made in the first paragraph?**
   (Rigorous) (Skill 11.6)

   A. The Eiffel Tower is in Paris, France but is enjoyed by the world

   B. The Eiffel Tower opened in 1889 and is still in the same spot today

   C. The Eiffel Tower is recognizable and it serves as a country's symbol

   D. The Eiffel Tower is a great symbol of France and a work of art

Answer: D. The Eiffel Tower is a great symbol of France and a work of art
The author is saying that the Eiffel Tower is both France's most recognized symbol and a work of art that was created in 1889 and is still in its original spot for all to enjoy.

6. **By using the word "luckily" in the final sentence of the first paragraph, what is the author implying?**
   (Rigorous) (Skill 10.1)

   A. That tearing the tower down as originally intended would have been a bad decision

   B. It is a good thing for France that the tower remains in the same spot it was built

   C. If the tower had been torn down, Gustave, its designer would have been angry

   D. The Universal Exhibition can now take place in the exact same spot someday since the tower remains

Answer: A. That tearing the tower down as originally intended would have been a bad decision
By using the transition word "luckily" to begin the last sentence in the first paragraph, the author is implying that it was a good decision to leave the tower in its original spot, and not destroy it as was originally planned, so that future generations might enjoy its artistic beauty.

7. **What words does the author use in paragraph 2 to clarify information for the reader?**
   (Average) (Skill 11.6)

   A. Between

   B. In order to

   C. Unfortunately

   D. In other words

Answer: D. In other words
The phrase *in other words* is a great transition that authors often use to clarify information stated in a previous sentence. Here, the author wants to draw the reader's attention to the fact that stairs do not run all the way to the top of the Eiffel Tower, and it is necessary for visitors to pay 13 francs to ride the elevator to the top.

8. **What would have been the best transition word for the author to use to connect these two sentences?**
   (Easy) (Skill 10.1)

   In order to ride to the second floor of the tower, a visitor must pay 8 francs to ride the elevator. To ride all the way to the top floor, a visitor must pay 13 francs.

   A.   Next,

   B.   Beyond,

   C.   For example,

   D.   Consequently,

Answer: D. Consequently,
Option A will not work because *next* is a transition word that shows time. *Beyond,* Option B, shows a place. Option C will not work because the author is not giving an example. However, Option D, *consequently,* is the best fit because it helps get the idea across that if visitors paid 8 francs to ride the elevator to the second floor, they would then have to pay a bit more to ride all the way to the top.

9. **What does the word "pang" mean in the sentence below?**
   (Easy) (Skill 10.3)

   Standing outside her homeroom, Lauren watched other children enter the room and overheard them sharing stories about their summer adventures. She couldn't help but feel a <u>pang</u> of loneliness as she thought of her best friend Morgan back in Colorado.

   A.   Pain

   B.   Hint

   C.   Depression

   D.   Song

Answer: B. Hint
The student feels a little bit lonely as she adjusts to a new school without her best friend from where she used to live.

10. What does the word "convoluted" mean in the sentence below?
(Easy) (Skill 10.3)

Misty listened to Marty intently. But as Marty revealed more of her plan, Misty wasn't sure she wanted anything to do with it. Marty's plan was <u>convoluted</u> and twisted and, quite frankly, Misty was worried about her own safety.

   A.   Strange

   B.   Straight

   C.   Thorough

   D.   Polluted

Answer: A. Strange
The author gives clarification for the word "convoluted" by adding the word "twisted" to the sentence. Therefore, the reader knows that the plan is strange and twisted because "strange" is a synonym of twisted in this context.

11. **The book *The Giver* by Lois Lowry is a great book. The characters are interesting and they are unique. Everyone who reads *The Giver* will enjoy it and not be able to put it down.**

   Is this a valid or invalid argument?
   (Average) (Skill 11.7)

   A.   Valid

   B.   Invalid

Answer: B. Invalid
The author does not support his opinions with any evidence or facts from the story.

12. I-95 is the best route to take from Virginia to Washington, DC. There are many rest stops along the way so it is easy to stop and get gas, buy food, and use the restrooms when necessary. There is also an HOV lane that allows those traveling with others to bypass single traveler cars.

Is this a valid or invalid argument?
(Average) (Skill 11.7)

A. Valid

B. Invalid

Answer: A. Valid
The author supports her opinions with evidence and facts.

DIRECTIONS: Read the following passage and answer the questions that follow.

This writer has often been asked to tutor hospitalized children with cystic fibrosis. While undergoing all the precautionary measures to see these children (for example, scrubbing thoroughly and donning a face mask and sterile gown), she has wondered why parents subject these children to the pressures of schooling and trying to catch up on what they have missed because of hospitalization, which is a normal part of cystic fibrosis patients' lives. These children undergo so many tortuous treatments a day that it seems cruel to expect them to learn as normal children do, especially when their life expectancies are so short.

13. **What type of organizational pattern does the author use?**
    (Rigorous) (Skill 11.2)

    A. Classification

    B. Example, clarification, and definition

    C. Comparison and contrast

    D. Cause and effect

Answer: B. Example, clarification, and definition
The author mentions tutoring children with cystic fibrosis in her opening sentence and goes on to explain and elaborate on her main idea. She focuses extensively on how little time the children have due to hospitalization and a shortened life span.

14. Is there evidence of bias in this paragraph?
(Rigorous) (Skill 11.3)

    A.   Yes

    B.   No

Answer: A. Yes
The writer clearly feels sorry for these children, and her writing reflects these personal feelings.

15. Elementary school is better than middle school.

Is this sentence a fact or an opinion?
(Easy) (Skill 11.3)

    A.   Fact

    B.   Opinion

Answer: B. Opinion
It depends on one's personal experience whether elementary or middle school is better.

16. Letter grades are given at Thomas Jefferson Middle School.

Is this sentence a fact or an opinion?
(Easy) (Skill 11.3)

    A.   Fact

    B.   Opinion

Answer: A. Fact
It can be proven whether Thomas Jefferson Middle School gives letter grades.

17. The science fair will take place at 4:00 on Saturday, March 13.

Is this sentence a fact or an opinion?
(Easy) (Skill 11.3)

A. Fact

B. Opinion

Answer: A. Fact
The time and place that something occurs is a fact because it can be proven.

18. The science fair will be a lot of fun so everyone should attend.

Is this sentence a fact or an opinion?
(Easy) (Skill 11.3)

A. Fact

B. Opinion

Answer: B. Opinion
It is up to individual attendees whether it was fun to attend the science fair. Therefore, it is an opinion.

19. Thank you so much for the gift you sent for my birthday. It was nice of you to send me a gift and remember that my birthday was last week. Your generosity is appreciated. Thanks again.

    John

    What conclusion can be drawn from the above letter?
    (Rigorous) (Skill 11.8)

    A. The author and the gift giver are related

    B. The author is a child that received a gift

    C. The gift was a toy and the author liked it

    D. The author didn't really like the gift

Answer: D. The author didn't really like the gift
Options A, B, and C might be true, but there isn't anything in the letter to support any of these ideas. Because nothing specific is addressed in the letter, it is acceptable to conclude that the author didn't really like the gift.

20. Even after I turned the lock correctly it still wouldn't open. My combination is 32-41-12; I hope this will help you get to the bottom of the problem. All of my school supplies are locked inside, and I must have them in order to be successful in my classes.

    What conclusion can be drawn from the paragraph above?
    (Average) (Skill 11.8)

    A. A teacher's belongings are locked inside of her car

    B. A student is having trouble with his locker

    C. A student's gym locker is jammed

    D. A traveler's locker is jammed

Answer: B. A student is having trouble with his locker
The student's class supplies are in their locker, which he can't open because of problems with the combination lock.

DIRECTIONS: Read the following passage and answer the questions that follow.

It is not news to anyone who has been following the changes in the economy that people are spending less. This is a wise decision by all consumers and since people are reevaluating their spending, it is necessary for companies to reevaluate their plans for growth. Many companies that were spending money on security have had to shift their focus elsewhere. A number of companies have made the decision to focus on virtualization—when one computer completes the jobs of many. Instead of a lot of computers doing a lot of jobs, one central, or main computer, will control all of the smaller jobs.

Due to the recession, companies are fighting for every little bit of business they can grab. Therefore, in today's rat race every little change might make a big difference. Companies believe that using one computer will save them money because one large computer can do more than one task at a time. Actually, it is considered the human version of multitasking. Furthermore, by moving toward virtualization, businesses can save energy. Businesses can reduce the number of computers, thus reducing the amount of energy that they use as a business, and saving additional time. With fewer machines there is less maintenance and time spent on maintenance can be spent elsewhere. With competition at an all-time high, small changes can make a big difference and virtualization meets this challenge that now faces the modern day business model. Only time will tell if the small change will have a big effect.

21. **How does the author feel about virtualization?**
    (Rigorous) (Skill 11.5)

    A. The author thinks that it is a great idea

    B. The author feels that it is the only way to handle the recession

    C. The author isn't convinced that the small change will have a big effect

    D. The author believes it should have been introduced a long time ago.

Answer: C. The author isn't convinced that the small change will have a big effect
The last sentence of the selection tells us that the author is not convinced that the small change will have a big effect on businesses.

22. How does the author feel about today's business environment?
    (Rigorous) (Skill 11.5)

    A. The author believes that it is difficult to succeed in today's business environment

    B. The author thinks that businesses have gotten too big

    C. The author feels that only people are capable of multi-tasking

    D. The author thinks that businesses rely too heavily on machines to do a human's work

Answer: A. The author believes that it is difficult to succeed in today's business environment
The first two sentences of the second paragraph use words like "fighting" and "rat race" to describe today's business environment. Therefore, you can tell that the author feels that it is difficult for businesses to succeed these days.

23. From this passage, one can infer that:
    (Rigorous) (Skill 11.8)

    A. The economy is doing well and companies are spending their money wisely

    B. The economy used to be doing better and consumers, as well as companies, have had to make adjustments

    C. The stock market is what drives consumer confidence and company sales

    D. Many companies do whatever other companies are doing

Answer: B. The economy used to be doing better and consumers, as well as companies, have had to make adjustments
This article is all about consumers and companies having to change the way they spend because of the status of the economy.

24. From this passage, one can infer that:
(Rigorous) (Skill 11.8)

    A.   Before the economy was doing poorly, companies focused their spending in other areas

    B.   Company workers are finding other jobs because of the bad economy

    C.   Employees will lose their jobs due to the recession

    D.   Companies are trying virtualization instead of resorting to employee layoffs to save money

Answer: A. Before the economy was doing poorly, companies focused their spending in other areas
Although B, C, and D are feasible choices, there isn't anything in the article that gives any indication that any of these choices would take place. Therefore, Option A is the best choice.

DIRECTIONS: Read the following passage and answer the questions that follow.

Megan was about to plant the last plant in the sunniest spot in the yard. She worked the soft, pliable soil to steady the plant around the roots. She filled in the empty area around the roots with more dirt. Recently, Megan had decided that she was going to plant a butterfly garden in her yard. She had worked very hard over the past week to clear the area so she would be able to plant this week while her grandparents were visiting. She and her grandmother had just returned from the nursery where they bought some petunias, peonies, and hollyhocks. Consequently, these plants would attract all sorts of butterflies.

25. **What is the main idea of the passage?**
    (Average) (Skill 10.1)

    A. How to create a butterfly garden

    B. Megan was in the final stages of creating her butterfly garden

    C. Petunias, peonies, and hollyhocks need to be planted in a sunny spot

    D. A butterfly garden is the name for a garden that contains peonies

Answer: B. Megan was in the final stages of creating her butterfly garden
The main idea of a fiction passage is also its summary. A good summary for this passage is Option B, "Megan was in the final stages of creating her butterfly garden."

26. **Why did the author write this article?**
    (Average) (Skill 11.1)

    A. To convince the reader to plant a butterfly garden

    B. To teach the reader how to plant a butterfly garden

    C. To encourage the reader to spend time with their family

    D. To amuse the reader with a story about planting a garden

Answer: D. To amuse the reader with a story about planting a garden
This was written to entertain. "Amuse" is a synonym for "entertain." Therefore, it is the best choice.

27. How is the passage organized?
    (Average) (Skill 11.2)

    A.   Sequence of events

    B.   Cause and effect

    C.   Statement support

    D.   Compare and contrast

Answer: A. Sequence of events
This narrative tells events in order.

28. What cause and effect relationship exists in this paragraph?
    (Rigorous) (Skill 11.6)

    A.   Because it is sunny, the butterflies will visit Megan's garden

    B.   Because Megan worked so hard this week, her grandparents came to visit

    C.   Because Megan planted certain plants, butterflies will like her garden

    D.   Because it was sunny, Megan was planting her last plant

Answer: C. Because Megan planted certain plants, butterflies will like her garden
Petunias, peonies, and hollyhocks are plants that attract butterflies. Because Megan planted these, butterflies will be attracted to her garden.

29. By using the word "consequently" in the final sentence of the first paragraph, what is the author implying?
    (Rigorous) (Skill 10.1)

    A. That Megan did not want butterflies to visit her garden

    B. Megan's grandmother did not want butterflies to visit the garden

    C. There would be consequences if the butterflies came to the garden

    D. The plants were purchased so that butterflies would visit the garden

Answer: D. The plants were purchased so that butterflies would visit the garden
Megan wants the butterflies to come to the garden and that is the reason that she purchased the types of plants that she did.

30. What transition word could the author have used to connect these two sentences?
    (Average) (Skill 10.1)

    She worked the soft, pliable soil to steady the plant around the roots. She filled in the empty area around the roots with more dirt.

    A. Third,

    B. Hence,

    C. Next,

    D. Prior to that,

Answer: C. Next,
"Next" shows time and works because Megan first settled the plant roots into the soil and then filled in the area around it. Options A and C won't work because they are not the correct sequence word. The word "hence" means "because."

31. What does the word "pliable" mean in the second sentence?
   (Average) (Skill 10.3)

   A. Wet

   B. Organic

   C. Bendable

   D. Sandy

Answer: C. Bendable
Megan was able to mold the soil around the roots of the plants because it was bendable.

DIRECTIONS: Read the following passage and answer the questions that follow.

The Fog and *The Hitchhiker* are both suspenseful. Both plays also contain ghost characters. Ghosts frighten me. *The Fog* has three ghost characters named Eben, Zeke, and a wounded man. The reader does not realize that these men are ghosts however, until the end of the play. In *The Hitchhiker*, there is one ghost character known as "The Gray Man" who stalks the main character, Ronald Adams, until the end of the play. It is not revealed however, who the hitchhiker is until the end. The reader needs to make their own decision about his significance. The Gray Man is a little creepy.
   The Fog takes place in Gettysburg, Pennsylvania during a war. *The Hitchhiker* on the other hand, is a more modern play and takes place during the 1930s and 1940s as a traveler drives to many cities across the country.

32. How is the passage organized?
   (Average) (Skill 11.2)

   A. Compare and contrast

   B. Cause and effect

   C. Sequence of events

   D. Statement support

Answer: A. Compare and contrast
This passage compares (gives similarities) and contrasts (shows differences) between two plays, *The Fog* and *The Hitchhiker.*

33. Which sentence in the passage is irrelevant?
   (Average) (Skill 11.6)

   A. *The Fog* and *The Hitchhiker* are both suspenseful.

   B. Both plays also contain ghost characters.

   C. Ghosts frighten me.

   D. *The Fog* has three ghost characters named Eben, Zeke, and a wounded man.

Answer: C. Ghosts frighten me.
The passage is talking about ghost characters that are in two plays. To interject personal feelings about ghosts is irrelevant.

34. Which sentence in the passage is irrelevant?
   (Rigorous) (Skill 11.6)

   A. The reader does not realize that these men are ghosts.

   B. In *The Hitchhiker*, there is one ghost character known as "The Gray Man."

   C. It is not revealed who the hitchhiker is until the end of the play.

   D. The Gray Man is a little creepy.

Answer: D. The Gray Man is a little creepy.
This is the author's personal opinion about the Gray Man and is irrelevant to the passage.

DIRECTIONS: Read the following passage and answer the questions that follow.

Smells were coming from the kitchen that repelled Kim further and further away. But he couldn't get far away enough to escape the odor. His sister Lee was experimenting with a new recipe. Lee often cooked new exotic and foreign dishes. Sometimes this was great for Kim because he was always the first one to try one of Lee's newest creations. He remembered the time that she made zesty fruit salsa with cinnamon pita chips. Maybe he could request that she make that again instead of what she was cooking now.

35. **What conclusion can be drawn from the passage?**
    (Rigorous) (Skill 11.8)

    A. Kim is a good cook

    B. Lee enjoys cooking

    C. Kim doesn't enjoy Lee's cooking

    D. Lee only makes desserts

Answer: B. Lee enjoys cooking
There isn't anything in the passage to support Options A and D. Option C isn't always true—we know that Kim enjoyed Lee's fruit salsa and cinnamon pita chips. Therefore, Option B is the best answer because the passage says that Lee likes to experiment in the kitchen.

36. **What can be inferred about Kim and Lee's relationship from the passage?**
    (Rigorous) (Skill 11.8)

    A. Overall, Kim and Lee get along

    B. Kim and Lee do not get along well

    C. Kim only tells Lee about dishes he doesn't like

    D. Kim and Lee only share an interest in cooking

Answer: A. Overall, Kim and Lee get along
It can be inferred from the passage that Kim and Lee have an overall good relationship. Lee enjoys cooking for Kim, and Kim enjoys trying Lee's experiments—most of the time.

DIRECTIONS: Read the following passage and answer the questions that follow.

Have you ever heard the expression "Busy as a bee"? Well, nothing could be truer. Bees are very busy insects, and they are very interesting. Bees live in colonies where each member has a specific job. In honeybee colonies, there are queens, drones, and workers. The queen is the largest bee and lays all the eggs. The drones do not have stingers, and their job is to mate with the queen. Most of the bees in the colony are workers. They care for the queen, remove trash, build the nest, guard the entrance, and collect nectar, pollen, and water. Sounds like most worker bees are males. The bees that go out to collect are called foragers.

37. What is the main idea of the passage?
   (Average) (Skill 10.1)

   A. Bees live in colonies

   B. There are three different types of bees

   C. Each type of bee has a specific job that is important to the colonies' survival

   D. Foragers are also known as collectors and they have an important job

Answer: C. Each type of bee has a specific job that is important to the colonies' survival
Options A, B, and D are all supporting details of the main idea, Option C.

38. What does the word "forage" mean?
   (Easy) (Skill 10.3)

   A. Work hard

   B. To be busy

   C. To care for

   D. Go and collect

Answer: D. Go and collect
The final sentence of the passage includes a context clue. It says, "The bees that go out to collect are called foragers."

39. Which is an opinion contained in this passage?
    (Average) (Skill 11.3)

    A.   Bees are very interesting

    B.   Bees live in colonies

    C.   Each colony has a queen

    D.   The queen is the largest bee

Answer: A. Bees are very interesting
Option A is the only choice that can be argued. Therefore, it is an opinion.

40. From this article you can see that the author thinks:
    (Rigorous) (Skill 11.5)

    A.   Bees lay large eggs

    B.   Drones have the best job

    C.   Male bees work very hard

    D.   Foragers have the most important job

Answer: C. Male bees work very hard
The author makes the statement "Sounds like most worker bees are males." By including this statement after naming many tasks that the worker bees perform, the author is stating his opinion about how much work the male bees do.

English Posttest

DIRECTIONS: Read the sentences and choose the best option that corrects an error in one of the underlined portions. If no error exists, choose "No change is necessary."

1. It will **definitely** be a great time and I am **positively** that everyone **who** attends will enjoy the party.
   (Average) (Skill 4.8)

   A. definite

   B. positive

   C. whom

   D. No change is necessary

2. There are **many** different **activities** planned for the day in all of the surrounding **communitys**.
   (Average) (Skill 4.10)

   A. much

   B. activitys

   C. communities

   D. No change is necessary

3. Jordan accepted **Chrises** invitation to go with him to the dance on Friday night.
   (Rigorous) (Skill 4.11)

   A. Chris's

   B. Chris'

   C. Chrises'

   D. No change is necessary

4. Michelle **was trying** to do her homework, but **he was making** too much noise.
   (Rigorous) (Skills 4.5 and 4.6)

   A. tried

   B. her brother

   C. made

   D. No change is necessary

5. When I returned home after running errands for the past hour, I wondered **whose** car was parked in my driveway.
   (Rigorous) (Skill 4.7)

   A. who's

   B. who is

   C. whos

   D. No change is necessary

6. **The expectations that have been put on <u>teachers</u> in the past few years <u>have grown</u> and <u>they</u> are very difficult to manage.**
   (Rigorous) (Skills 4.4 and 4.6)

   A. teacher's

   B. has grown

   C. these expectations

   D. No change is necessary

7. **Austin <u>was watching</u> television on the couch when his dad <u>looked</u> at him with an encouraging look. "I <u>has taken</u> out the trash already," Austin said.**
   (Average) (Skills 4.1 and 4.4)

   A. had watched

   B. looking

   C. have taken

   D. Not change is necessary

8. **<u>Christian Montgomery</u> <u>our honorable mayor</u> will be leading us in the <u>ceremonies</u> that day.**
   (Rigorous) (Skill 4.11)

   A. Christian montgomery

   B. Christian Montgomery, our honorable mayor,

   C. Ceremonies

   D. No change is necessary

9. **Pizza tastes <u>more better</u> when you <u>put cheese</u>, mushrooms, and onions all over the top of it.**
   (Easy) (Skill 4.9)

   A. better

   B. putt

   C. cheesy

   D. No change is necessary

10. **The lemonade that <u>was being</u> sold at the <u>children's</u> lemonade stand was <u>more sweet</u> than the iced tea.**
    (Rigorous) (Skill 4.9)

    A. has been

    B. childrens

    C. sweeter

    D. No change is necessary

115

11. The <u>students</u> and the <u>teachers</u> <u>is</u> going to attend the performance at noon on Thursday.
    (Easy) (Skill 4.3)

    A. student's

    B. teachers'

    C. are

    D. No change is necessary

12. After the town was evacuated <u>due to</u> expected strong <u>storms, I</u> reported to the authorities that there <u>wasn't nobody</u> left in our whole house.
    (Average) (Skill 4.4)

    A. because of

    B. storms I

    C. wasn't anybody

    D. No change is necessary

13. This weekend we are going to <u>mow</u> the <u>lawn, wash</u> the windows, and <u>trimming</u> the shrubs.
    (Easy) (Skill 3.2)

    A. mowing

    B. lawn; wash

    C. trim

    D. No change is necessary

14. The local meteorologists <u>are</u> forecasting <u>neither</u> rain <u>or</u> snow for the holiday week.
    (Rigorous) (Skill 3.2)

    A. is

    B. niether

    C. nor

    D. No change is necessary

15. We will <u>be celebrating</u> the <u>Fourth of July</u> at <u>independence park</u> located in the center of Gorham Township.
    (Average) (Skill 4.12)

    A. celebrating

    B. fourth of July

    C. Independence Park

    D. No change is necessary

DIRECTIONS: In each of the following sentences, some part of the sentence or the entire sentence is underlined. Beneath each sentence you will find four ways of rewriting the underlined part. Select the best answer that will make the sentence correct.

16. **The states of Oklahoma, Texas, and Missouri were severe affected by the drought caused from a lack of rain this summer.**
    (Average) (Skill 4.8)

    A. The states of Oklahoma, Texas, and Missouri were more severely affected by the drought caused from a lack of rain this summer.

    B. The states of Oklahoma, Texas, and Missouri was severely affected by the drought caused from a lack of rain this summer.

    C. The states of Oklahoma, Texas, and Missouri were severely affected by the drought caused from a lack of rain this summer.

    D. No change is necessary

17. **Who do you think has the neatest handwriting in the class?**
    (Rigorous) (Skill 4.7)

    A. Whom do you think have the neater handwriting in the class?

    B. Who do you think have the neatest handwriting in the class?

    C. Who do you think has the neatest handwriting in the class.

    D. No change is necessary

18. **The professor and his assistant presented they're report at the annual conference of financial economic stimulus representatives.**
(Average) (Skill 2.2)

A. The professor and his assistant presented its report at the annual conference of financial economic stimulus representatives.

B. The professor and his assistant presented theirs report at the annual conference of financial economic stimulus representatives.

C. The professor and his assistant presented their report at the annual conference of financial economic stimulus representatives.

D. No change is necessary

19. **Since its supposed to rain today I think its best if you take your umbrella.**
(Average) (Skill 4.11)

A. Since it's supposed to rain today, I think its best if you take you're umbrella.

B. Since it's supposed to rain today, I think it's best if you take your umbrella.

C. Since its supposed to rain today I think its best if you take you're umbrella.

D. No change is necessary

20. **Our regularly scheduled meeting will be hold on Tuesday, March 11 at 3:00 that afternoon.**
(Easy) (Skill 4.2)

A. Our regular scheduled meeting will be hold on Tuesday, March 11 at 3:00 in the afternoon.

B. Our regularly scheduled meeting will be held on Tuesday, March 11 at 3:00 in the afternoon.

C. Are regularly scheduled meeting will be held on Tuesday, March 11 at 3:00 that afternoon.

D. No change is necessary

21. **The frog eggs were laid a few weeks ago, so they have been hatching soon.**
    (Easy) (Skill 4.2)

    A. The frog eggs were laid a few weeks ago, so they will be hatching soon.

    B. The frog eggs were laid a few weeks ago, so they is hatching soon.

    C. The frog eggs were laid a few weeks ago, so they be done hatching soon.

    D. No change is necessary

22. **We were supposed to work on a project for school, but after an hour we started to get hungry and deciding to make popcorn.**
    (Average) (Skill 4.2)

    A. We were supposed to work on a project for school, but after an hour we started to get hungry and were deciding to make popcorn.

    B. We were supposed to work on a project for school, but after an hour we started to get hungry and decide to make popcorn.

    C. We were supposed to work on a project for school, but after an hour we started to get hungry and decided to make popcorn.

    D. No change is necessary

23. **I had brought home some movies from the video store but not anybody wanted to watch them so we played a game instead.**
    (Average) (Skill 4.5)

    A. I brought home some movies from the video store but not anyone wanted to watch them so we played a game instead.

    B. I brought home some movies from the video store but nobody wanted to watch them so we played a game instead.

    C. I brought home some movies from the video store but somebody wanted to watch them so we played a game instead.

    D. No change is necessary

24. **Coloring hard-boiled eggs is an Easter tradition that many people still follow today.**
    (Rigorous) (Skill 3.3)

    A. that many people followed today

    B. that many people following today

    C. that much peoples follow today

    D. No change is necessary

25. **Temperatures are rising, <u>yet the trees are blooming and the grass is quickly growing.</u>**
    (Rigorous) (Skill 1.1)

    A. but the trees is blooming and the grass is quickly growing

    B. and the trees are blooming and the grass is quickly growing

    C. yet, the trees are blooming and the grass is quickly growing

    D. No change is necessary

26. **<u>In my opinion we would all be much better off if there were less choices in the grocery stores.</u> There seems to be an overabundance of choice and it is confusing to some.**
    (Rigorous) (Skill 2.1)

    A. In my opinion, we should all be much more better off is there was less choices in the grocery stores.

    B. In my opinion, we would all be better off if there were less choices in the grocery stores.

    C. In my opinion we would all be much better off if there were fewer choices in the grocery stores.

    D. No change is necessary

27. **<u>Supposably, the keynote speaker at the annual convention is an alumni of Princeton University.</u>**
    (Average) (Skill 2.1)

    A. Supposedly, the keynote speaker at the annual convention is an alumnus of Princeton University.

    B. Supposably the keynote speaker, at the annual convention, is an alumni of Princeton University.

    C. Supposably, the keynote speaker during the annual convention was an alumnus at Princeton University.

    D. No change is necessary

28. **<u>I was not expecting to except his advice but it actually made sense and solved the problem.</u>**
    (Rigorous) (Skill 2.2)

    A. I was not expecting to except his advise, but it actually made sense and solved the problem.

    B. I was not expecting to accept his advice but it actually made sense and solved the problem.

    C. I was not expecting to except his advice since it actually made sense and solved the problem.

    D. No change is necessary

29. **When children are learning to read, they often read allowed in order to assist with monitoring their own comprehension.**
(Average) (Skill 2.2)

   A. When children is learning to read, we often read allowed in order to assist with monitoring their own comprehension.

   B. When children are learning to read, they often read aloud in order to assist with monitoring their own comprehension.

   C. When children are learning to read, she often read allowed in order to assist with monitor there own comprehension.

   D. No change is necessary

30. **Many northern residents are choosing to immigrate to the south to take advantage of lower taxes and nicer weather.**
(Rigorous) (Skill 2.2)

   A. Many Northern residents are choosing to immigrate to the South to take advantage of lower taxes and nicer weather.

   B. Many northern residents choosed to immigrate to the south to take advantage of lower taxes and nicer weather.

   C. Many northern residents are choosing to emigrate to the south to take advantage of lower taxes and nicer weather.

   D. No change is necessary

31. **When I was younger, my family and I used to go to visit my grandparents for the summer at their home in North Carolina.**
(Rigorous) (Skill 4.1)

   A. When I was younger, my family and I use to go to visit my grandparents for the summer at their home in North Carolina.

   B. When I was younger, my family and me used to go to visit my Grandparent's for the summer at their home in North Carolina.

   C. When I was younger my family and us used to go to visit my grandparents for the summer at there home in North Carolina.

   D. No change is necessary

32. **Maurice put together a good presentation in class and he did good.**
(Average) (Skill 4.8)

   A. Maurice put together a good presentation in class and he did well.

   B. Maurice put together a well presentation in class and he did well.

   C. Maurice put together a well presentation in class and he did good.

   D. No change is necessary

33. **I can't believe that you didn't see that red light that was so oblivious.**
(Easy) (Skills 1.3 and 2.2)

   A. I can't believe that you didn't see that red light that was so enormous.

   B. I can't believe that you didn't see that red light that was so relevant.

   C. I can't believe that you didn't see that red light that was so obvious.

   D. No change is necessary

34. **My lunchbox contained many different treats; cookies, fruit, nuts, and cheese.**
(Rigorous) (Skill 4.11)

   A. My lunchbox contained many different treats: cookies, fruit, nuts, and cheese.

   B. My lunchbox contained many different treats, cookies, fruit, nuts and cheese.

   C. My lunchbox contained many different treats. cookies, fruit, nuts and cheese.

   D. No change is necessary.

35. **After the rain stopped many turtles sat sunning themselves.** *(Average) (Skill 4.11)*

    A. After the rain stopped, much turtles sat sunning themselves.

    B. After the rain stopped, many turtles sat sunning theirselves.

    C. After the rain stopped, many turtles sat sunning themselves.

    D. No change is necessary

36. **I have just finished the book, "The Lion king," and I would recommend it to anyone who enjoys a good mystery.** *(Average) (Skills 4.11 and 4.12)*

    A. I have just finished the book *The Lion King,* and I would recommend it to anyone who enjoys a good mystery.

    B. I have just finished the book *the Lion King* and I would recommend it to anyone who enjoys a good mystery.

    C. I have just finished the book, "the lion king" and I would recommend it to anyone who enjoys a good mystery.

    D. No change is necessary

DIRECTIONS: Read the following passage and answer the questions that follow.

Davy Crockett grew up in Tennessee. When he was just a young boy he learned to hunt, fish, and drive cattle. At twelve years old, he traveled three hundred miles to complete a cattle drive. Davy's father thought school was important, but Davy did not agree. He left home and did not return until he was fifteen. He had grown to nearly six feet tall. When he returned, he was employed by a farmer whose son taught school. It was because of this fact that Davy developed a new interest in reading and writing. Davy also developed another interest—shooting rifles and hunting animals. He often missed his mother. Legend has it that Davy had very good aim and captured more than 100 bears in just a six-month period.

37. **Which sentence in the passage is irrelevant?** *(Average) (Skill 1.2)*

    A. Davy Crockett grew up in Tennessee.

    B. When he was just a young boy he learned to hunt, fish, and drive cattle.

    C. He had grown to nearly six feet tall.

    D. Legend has it that Davy had very good aim.

38. Which sentence in the passage is irrelevant?
    (Easy) (Skill 1.2)

    A. Davy also developed another interest.

    B. He often missed his mother.

    C. Legend has it that Davy had very good aim.

    D. Davy captured more than 100 bears in just six months.

DIRECTIONS: In each of the following sentences, some part of the sentence or the entire sentence is underlined. Beneath each sentence you will find four ways of rewriting the underlined part. Select the best answer that will make the sentence correct.

39. Walt Whitman was famous for <u>his composition, *Leaves of Grass*, serving as a nurse during the Civil War, and a devoted son.</u>
    (Rigorous) (Skill 2.2)

    A. *Leaves of Grass*, his service as a nurse during the Civil War, and a devoted son.

    B. composing *Leaves of Grass*, serving as a nurse during the Civil War, and being a devoted son.

    C. his composition, *Leaves of Grass*, his nursing during the Civil War, and his devotion as a son.

    D. No change is necessary

40. A teacher <u>must know not only her subject matter</u> but also the strategies of content teaching. *(Rigorous) (Skill 3.1)*

   A. must not only know her subject matter

   B. not only must know her subject matter

   C. must not know only her subject matter

   D. No change is necessary

Answer Key: English Posttest

1. B
2. C
3. A
4. B
5. D
6. C
7. C
8. B
9. A
10. C
11. C
12. C
13. C
14. C
15. C
16. C
17. D
18. C
19. B
20. B
21. A
22. C
23. B
24. D
25. B
26. C
27. A
28. B
29. B
30. C
31. D
32. A
33. C
34. A
35. C
36. A
37. C
38. B
39. B
40. D

Rigor Table: English Posttest

	Easy 20%	Average 39%	Rigorous 41%
Questions	9, 11, 13, 20, 21, 33, 37, 38	1, 2, 7, 12, 15, 16, 18, 19, 22, 23, 27, 29, 32, 35, 36	3, 4, 5, 6, 8, 10, 14, 17, 24, 25, 26, 28, 30, 31, 34, 39, 40

Posttest with Rationales: English

DIRECTIONS: Read the sentences and choose the best option that corrects an error in one of the underlined portions. If no error exists, choose "No change is necessary."

1. It will <u>definitely</u> be a great time and I am <u>positively</u> that everyone <u>who</u> attends will enjoy the party.
   (Average) (Skill 4.8)

   A.   definite

   B.   positive

   C.   whom

   D.   No change is necessary

Answer: B. positive
The adverb "positively" is used incorrectly in the sentence. The adjectival form "positive" is correct.

2. There are <u>many</u> different <u>activities</u> planned for the day in all of the surrounding <u>communitys</u>.
   (Average) (Skill 4.10)

   A.   much

   B.   activitys

   C.   communities

   D.   No change is necessary

Answer: C. communities
The word "communities" is spelled incorrectly.

3. **Jordan accepted <u>Chrises</u> invitation to go with him to the dance on Friday night.**
   (Rigorous) (Skill 4.11)

    A. Chris's

    B. Chris'

    C. Chrises'

    D. No change is necessary

Answer: A. Chris's
The sentence indicates possession—or Chris is the owner of the invitation. Therefore, an apostrophe and *s* are needed to show ownership.

4. **Michelle <u>was trying</u> to do her homework, but <u>he was making</u> too much noise.**
   (Rigorous) (Skills 4.5 and 4.6)

    A. tried

    B. her brother

    C. made

    D. No change is necessary

Answer: B. her brother
The pronoun "he" cannot be used because the only noun that appears in the sentence so far is Michelle, and "he" cannot be the pronoun to take the place of Michelle. More clarification is needed as to who "he" is.

5. **When I returned home after running errands for the past hour, I wondered <u>whose</u> car was parked in my driveway.**
   (Rigorous) (Skill 4.7)

   A.   who's

   B.   who is

   C.   whos

   D.   No change is necessary

   Answer: D. No change is necessary
   The word "whose" is the correct form of the word for this situation.

6. **The expectations that have been put on <u>teachers</u> in the past few years <u>have grown</u> and <u>they</u> are very difficult to manage.**
   (Rigorous) (Skills 4.4 and 4.6)

   A.   teacher's

   B.   has grown

   C.   these expectations

   D.   No change is necessary

   Answer: C. these expectations
   The pronoun "they" is not clearly identified. It can be replacing either the teachers or the expectations. Clarification is needed, as in Option C, rather than simply using the pronoun "they."

7. Austin <u>was watching</u> television on the couch when his dad <u>looked</u> at him with an encouraging look. "I <u>has taken</u> out the trash already," Austin said.
   (Average) (Skills 4.1 and 4.4)

   A.   had watched

   B.   looking

   C.   have taken

   D.   No change is necessary

Answer: C. have taken
The past participle of the verb to take is taken, and "have" is the correct helping verb for the pronoun "I."

8. **Christian Montgomery our honorable mayor will be leading us in the ceremonies that day.**
   (Rigorous) (Skill 4.11)

   A.   Chritian montgomery

   B.   Christian Montgomery, our honorable mayor,

   C.   Ceremonies

   D.   No change is necessary

Answer: B. Christian Montgomery, our honorable mayor,
Commas are needed to separate the dependent clause, our honorable mayor. We know this is a dependent clause because if it were removed from the sentence, the sentence would still make sense.

9. **Pizza tastes <u>more better</u> when you <u>put cheese</u>, mushrooms, and onions all over the top of it.**
(Easy) (Skill 4.9)

   A. better

   B. putt

   C. cheesy

   D. No change is necessary

Answer: A. better
More better is an incorrect adjective. The correct adjective needed is simply "better."

10. **The lemonade that <u>was being</u> sold at the <u>children's</u> lemonade stand was <u>more sweet</u> than the iced tea.**
(Rigorous) (Skill 4.9)

   A. has been

   B. childrens

   C. sweeter

   D. No change is necessary

Answer: C. sweeter
The correct word to use when comparing sweet items is "sweeter," not "more sweet." All of the other choices are correct in the sentence.

11. The <u>students</u> and the <u>teachers</u> <u>is</u> going to attend the performance at noon on Thursday.
    (Easy) (Skill 4.3)

    A.   student's

    B.   teachers'

    C.   are

    D.   No change is necessary

Answer: C. are
The linking verb agreement must correspond with the plurality of the subjects. The subjects are the students and the teachers; this is a compound subject. Therefore, "are" is needed to correspond with these subjects.

12. After the town was evacuated <u>due to</u> expected strong <u>storms, I</u> reported to the authorities that there <u>wasn't nobody</u> left in our whole house.
    (Average) (Skill 4.4)

    A.   because of

    B.   storms I

    C.   wasn't anybody

    D.   No change is necessary

Answer: C. wasn't anybody
"Wasn't nobody" is a double negative and is an error. Two forms of negation cannot be used together in a sentence. The correct word to use with "wasn't" is "anybody."

13. This weekend we are going to <u>mow</u> the <u>lawn, wash</u> the windows, and <u>trimming</u> the shrubs.
    (Easy) (Skill 3.2)

    A. mowing

    B. lawn; wash

    C. trim

    D. No change is necessary

Answer: C. trim
The sentence is in the future tense, "are going," and lists the first two things that need be done as "mow the lawn" and "wash the windows." Therefore, the last item, "trim the shrubs," needs to stay parallel with the two items listed first.

14. The local meteorologists <u>are</u> forecasting <u>neither</u> rain <u>or</u> snow for the holiday week.
    (Rigorous) (Skill 3.2)

    A. is

    B. niether

    C. nor

    D. No change is necessary

Answer: C. nor
The correlative conjunction "neither" is used. Therefore, when "neither" is used, "nor" must follow—not "or." "Or" is used in correlation with the word "either."

15. We will be celebrating the Fourth of July at independence park located in the center of Gorham Township.
    (Average) (Skill 4.12)

    A.   celebrating

    B.   fourth of July

    C.   Independence Park

    D.   No change is necessary

Answer: C. Independence Park
Independence Park is the proper name of a specific park and therefore must be capitalized.

DIRECTIONS: In each of the following sentences, some part of the sentence or the entire sentence is underlined. Beneath each sentence you will find four ways of rewriting the underlined part. Select the best answer that will make the sentence correct.

16. The states of Oklahoma, Texas, and Missouri were severe affected by the drought caused from a lack of rain this summer.
    (Average) (Skill 4.8)

    A.   The states of Oklahoma, Texas, and Missouri were more severely affected by the drought caused from a lack of rain this summer.

    B.   The states of Oklahoma, Texas, and Missouri was severely affected by the drought caused from a lack of rain this summer.

    C.   The states of Oklahoma, Texas, and Missouri were severely affected by the drought caused from a lack of rain this summer.

    D.   No change is necessary

Answer: C. The states of Oklahoma, Texas, and Missouri were severely affected by the drought caused from a lack of rain this summer.
The adverb "severely" is needed to describe how the three states were affected by the lack of rain this summer.

17. **Who do you think has the neatest handwriting in the class?**
    (Rigorous) (Skill 4.7)

    A. Whom do you think have the neater handwriting in the class?

    B. Who do you think have the neatest handwriting in the class?

    C. Who do you think has the neatest handwriting in the class.

    D. No change is necessary

Answer: D. No change is necessary
The original sentence is written and punctuated correctly. No changes are needed. The statement is a question and therefore requires a question mark.

18. **The professor and his assistant presented they're report at the annual conference of financial economic stimulus representatives.**
    (Average) (Skill 2.2)

    A. The professor and his assistant presented its report at the annual conference of financial economic stimulus representatives.

    B. The professor and his assistant presented theirs report at the annual conference of financial economic stimulus representatives.

    C. The professor and his assistant presented their report at the annual conference of financial economic stimulus representatives.

    D. No change is necessary

Answer: C. The professor and his assistant presented their report at the annual conference of financial economic stimulus representatives.
The report belongs to the professor and his assistant. Therefore, the correct pronoun to use is "their."

19. Since its supposed to rain today I think its best if you take your umbrella.
   (Average) (Skill 4.11)

   A. Since it's supposed to rain today, I think its best if you take you're umbrella.

   B. Since it's supposed to rain today, I think it's best if you take your umbrella.

   C. Since its supposed to rain today I think its best if you take you're umbrella.

   D. No change is necessary

Answer: B. Since it's supposed to rain today, I think it's best if you take your umbrella.
There were three words to examine closely in this sentence: "its," "its," and "your." "It's" is the contraction for the two words it + is. "Its" shows possession. "You're" is the contraction for the two words you + are. If the contraction does not work in the sentence, for example, "take *you are* umbrella," then the contraction is not grammatically correct.

20. Our regularly scheduled meeting will be hold on Tuesday, March 11 at 3:00 that afternoon.
   (Easy) (Skill 4.2)

   A. Our regular scheduled meeting will be hold on Tuesday, March 11 at 3:00 in the afternoon.

   B. Our regularly scheduled meeting will be held on Tuesday, March 11 at 3:00 in the afternoon.

   C. Are regularly scheduled meeting will be held on Tuesday, March 11 at 3:00 that afternoon.

   D. No change is necessary

Answer: B. Our regularly scheduled meeting will be held on Tuesday, March 11 at 3:00 in the afternoon.
The word "hold" needs to be "held" because of the way the sentence is worded. If it were, "We will *hold* our regularly scheduled meeting..." then the verb would have to be "hold" to indicate the future tense.

21. The frog eggs were laid a few weeks ago, so they have been hatching soon.
    (Easy) (Skill 4.2)

    A. The frog eggs were laid a few weeks ago, so they will be hatching soon.

    B. The frog eggs were laid a few weeks ago, so they is hatching soon.

    C. The frog eggs were laid a few weeks ago, so they be done hatching soon.

    D. No change is necessary

Answer: A. The frog eggs were laid a few weeks ago, so they will be hatching soon.
The correct tense form of the verb that is needed is the future.

22. We were supposed to work on a project for school, but after an hour we started to get hungry and deciding to make popcorn.
    (Average) (Skill 4.2)

    A. We were supposed to work on a project for school, but after an hour we started to get hungry and were deciding to make popcorn.

    B. We were supposed to work on a project for school, but after an hour we started to get hungry and dedide to make popcorn.

    C. We were supposed to work on a project for school, but after an hour we started to get hungry and decided to make popcorn.

    D. No change is necessary

Answer: C. We were supposed to work on a project for school, but after an hour we started to get hungry and decided to make popcorn.
The sentence is written in the past tense and therefore must remain in the past tense. Therefore, the verb "decided" is needed to make the sentence grammatically correct.

23. I had brought home some movies from the video store but not anybody wanted to watch them so we played a game instead.
   (Average)(Skill 4.5)

   A. I brought home some movies from the video store but not anyone wanted to watch them so we played a game instead.

   B. I brought home some movies from the video store but nobody wanted to watch them so we played a game instead.

   C. I brought home some movies from the video store but somebody wanted to watch them so we played a game instead.

   D. No change is necessary

Answer: B. I brought home some movies from the video store but nobody wanted to watch them so we played a game instead.
All of the sentences contain double negatives except Option B. The correct term is "nobody."

24. Coloring hard-boiled eggs is an Easter tradition <u>that many people still follow today</u>.
   (Rigorous) (Skill 3.3)

   A. that many people followed today

   B. that many people following today

   C. that much peoples follow today

   D. No change is necessary

Answer: D. No change is necessary
The way the sentence is written is correct and no changes are necessary.

25. **Temperatures are rising, yet the trees are blooming and the grass is quickly growing.**
   (Rigorous) (Skill 1.1)

   A.   but the trees is blooming and the grass is quickly growing

   B.   and the trees are blooming and the grass is quickly growing

   C.   yet, the trees are blooming and the grass is quickly growing

   D.   No change is necessary

   Answer: B. and the trees are blooming and the grass is quickly growing
   This is a cause and effect sentence. Because the temperatures are rising, the trees are blooming and the grass is quickly growing. Therefore, a connecting word like "and" is needed rather than a contradictory word like "but" or "yet."

26. **In my opinion we would all be much better off if there were less choices in the grocery stores. There seems to be an overabundance of choice and it is confusing to some.**
   (Rigorous) (Skill 2.1)

   A.   In my opinion, we should all be much more better off is there was less choices in the grocery stores.

   B.   In my opinion, we would all be better off if there were less choices in the grocery stores.

   C.   In my opinion we would all be much better off if there were fewer choices in the grocery stores.

   D.   No change is necessary

   Answer: C. In my opinion we would all be much better off if there were fewer choices in the grocery stores.
   The only word that must be changed in the original sentence is "less" to "fewer." "Less" is used to answer the question, "How much?" whereas "fewer" is used to answer the question, "How many?"

27. Supposably, the keynote speaker at the annual convention is an alumni of Princeton University.
    (Average) (Skills 2.1 and 4.10)

    A.   Supposedly, the keynote speaker at the annual convention is an alumnus of Princeton University.

    B.   Supposably the keynote speaker, at the annual convention, is an alumni of Princeton University.

    C.   Supposably, the keynote speaker during the annual convention was an alumnus at Princeton University.

    D.   No change is necessary

Answer: A. Supposedly, the keynote speaker at the annual convention is an alumnus of Princeton University.
The other choices are automatically incorrect, because "supposably" is incorrect. The correct word is "supposedly." Options A and C also correct the spelling "alumni," which is the plural form of alumnus.

28. I was not expecting to except his advice but it actually made sense and solved the problem.
    (Rigorous) (Skill 2.2)

    A.   I was not expecting to except his advise, but it actually made sense and solved the problem.

    B.   I was not expecting to accept his advice but it actually made sense and solved the problem.

    C.   I was not expecting to except his advice since it actually made sense and solved the problem.

    D.   No change is necessary

Answer: B. I was not expecting to accept his advice but it actually made sense and solved the problem.
The only problem with the original sentence is the word "except," which means "excluding." This sentence calls for the word "accept" which means "to receive or to tolerate."

29. **When children are learning to read, they often read allowed in order to assist with monitoring their own comprehension.**
    (Average) (Skill 2.2)

    A. When children is learning to read, we often read allowed in order to assist with monitoring their own comprehension.

    B. When children are learning to read, they often read aloud in order to assist with monitoring their own comprehension.

    C. When children are learning to read, she often read allowed in order to assist with monitor there own comprehension.

    D. No change is necessary

Answer: B. When children are learning to read, they often read aloud in order to assist with monitoring their own comprehension.
The only error in the original sentence is with the word "allowed," which means "permitted." The word needed here is "aloud," an adverb that means "audible or able to be heard."

30. **Many northern residents are choosing to immigrate to the south to take advantage of lower taxes and nicer weather.**
    (Rigorous) (Skill 2.2)

    A. Many Northern residents are choosing to immigrate to the South to take advantage of lower taxes and nicer weather.

    B. Many northern residents choosed to immigrate to the south to take advantage of lower taxes and nicer weather.

    C. Many northern residents are choosing to emigrate to the south to take advantage of lower taxes and nicer weather.

    D. No change is necessary

Answer: C. Many northern residents are choosing to emigrate to the south to take advantage of lower taxes and nicer weather.
The only error in the original sentence is the word "immigrate," which means "to enter another country and reside there." In this sentence, residents are choosing to leave and settle in another region, which is "emigrate."

31. When I was younger, my family and I used to go to visit my grandparents for the summer at their home in North Carolina. *(Rigorous) (Skill 4.1)*

    A. When I was younger, my family and I use to go to visit my grandparents for the summer at their home in North Carolina.

    B. When I was younger, my family and me used to go to visit my Grandparent's for the summer at their home in North Carolina.

    C. When I was younger my family and us used to go to visit my grandparents for the summer at there home in North Carolina.

    D. No change is necessary

Answer: D. No change is necessary
The sentence is correct the way it is written but there are many places to check. First, the correct wording is "used to." Next, "my family and I" is written correctly. A way to check is to omit "my family" and try the sentence that way. "I used to go... me used to go..." Choose the one that is grammatically correct. Finally, the correct form is "their" home since it shows possession.

32. Maurice put together a good presentation in class and he did good. *(Average) (Skill 4.8)*

    A. Maurice put together a good presentation in class and he did well.

    B. Maurice put together a well presentation in class and he did well.

    C. Maurice put together a well presentation in class and he did good.

    D. No change is necessary

Answer: A. Maurice put together a good presentation in class and he did well.
Describing the presentation requires the word "good." However, when describing the effort level someone has shown, the word "well" is needed.

33. I can't believe that you didn't see that red light that was so oblivious.
(Easy) (Skills 1.3 and 2.2)

 A. I can't believe that you didn't see that red light that was so enormous.

 B. I can't believe that you didn't see that red light that was so relevant.

 C. I can't believe that you didn't see that red light that was so obvious.

 D. No change is necessary

Answer: C. I can't believe that you didn't see that red light that was so obvious.
The correct word here to be used is "obvious."

34. My lunchbox contained many different treats; cookies, fruit, nuts, and cheese.
(Rigorous) (Skill 4.11)

 A. My lunchbox contained many different treats: cookies, fruit, nuts, and cheese.

 B. My lunchbox contained many different treats, cookies, fruit, nuts and cheese.

 C. My lunchbox contained many different treats. cookies, fruit, nuts and cheese.

 D. No change is necessary

Answer: A. My lunchbox contained many different treats: cookies, fruit, nuts, and cheese.
The correct punctuation mark to use before a series of items listed and separated by commas is the colon. In addition, a comma is required between the words "nuts" and "cheese" because there are items listed in a series.

35. After the rain stopped many turtles sat sunning themselves.
    (Average) (Skill 4.11)

    A.   After the rain stopped, much turtles sat sunning themselves.

    B.   After the rain stopped, many turtles sat sunning theirselves.

    C.   After the rain stopped, many turtles sat sunning themselves.

    D.   No change is necessary

Answer: C. After the rain stopped, many turtles sat sunning themselves.
The dependent clause "After the rain stopped" requires a comma afterward. "Many" is used to describe the number of turtles because they could be counted. Also, "themselves" is the correct word.

36. I have just finished the book, "The Lion king," and I would recommend it to anyone who enjoys a good mystery.
    (Average) (Skills 4.11 and 4.12)

    A.   I have just finished the book *The Lion King,* and I would recommend it to anyone who enjoys a good mystery.

    B.   I have just finished the book *the Lion King* and I would recommend it to anyone who enjoys a good mystery.

    C.   I have just finished the book, "the lion king" and I would recommend it to anyone who enjoys a good mystery.

    D.   No change is necessary

Answer: A. I have just finished the book *The Lion King,* and I would recommend it to anyone who enjoys a good mystery.
The comma is needed to separate two independent clauses. If a book title is typed, then it should be in italics. If the title is handwritten, it should be underlined. Every main word of the title must be capitalized.

DIRECTIONS: Read the following passage and answer the questions that follow.

Davy Crockett grew up in Tennessee. When he was just a young boy he learned to hunt, fish, and drive cattle. At twelve years old, he traveled three hundred miles to complete a cattle drive. Davy's father thought school was important, but Davy did not agree. He left home and did not return until he was fifteen. He had grown to nearly six feet tall. When he returned, he was employed by a farmer whose son taught school. It was because of this fact that Davy developed a new interest in reading and writing. Davy also developed another interest—shooting rifles and hunting animals. He often missed his mother. Legend has it that Davy had very good aim and captured more than 100 bears in just a six-month period.

37. **Which sentence in the passage is irrelevant?**
    (Easy) (Skill 1.2)

    A. Davy Crockett grew up in Tennessee.

    B. When he was just a young boy he learned to hunt, fish, and drive cattle.

    C. He had grown to nearly six feet tall.

    D. Legend has it that Davy had very good aim.

Answer: C. He had grown to nearly six feet tall
The fact that Davy had grown to nearly six feet tall is not necessary to the paragraph.

38. **Which sentence in the passage is irrelevant?**
    (Average) (Skill 1.2)

    A. Davy also developed another interest.

    B. He often missed his mother.

    C. Legend has it that Davy had very good aim.

    D. Davy captured more than 100 bears in just six months.

Answer: B. He often missed his mother.
The idea that Davy often missed his mother does not fit in where it is in the paragraph—it is irrelevant.

DIRECTIONS: In each of the following sentences, some part of the sentence or the entire sentence is underlined. Beneath each sentence you will find four ways of rewriting the underlined part. Select the best answer that will make the sentence correct.

39. Walt Whitman was famous for <u>his composition, *Leaves of Grass*, serving as a nurse during the Civil War, and a devoted son.</u>
    (Rigorous) (Skill 3.2)

    A. *Leaves of Grass*, his service as a nurse during the Civil War, and a devoted son.

    B. composing *Leaves of Grass*, serving as a nurse during the Civil War, and being a devoted son.

    C. his composition, *Leaves of Grass*, his nursing during the Civil War, and his devotion as a son.

    D. No change is necessary

Answer: B. composing *Leaves of Grass*, serving as a nurse during the Civil War, and being a devoted son
In order to have a parallel structure, the sentence needs three gerunds. The other sentences use both gerunds and nouns and therefore lack parallelism.

40. A teacher <u>must know not only her subject matter</u> but also the strategies of content teaching.
    (Rigorous) (Skill 3.1)

    A. must not only know her subject matter

    B. not only must know her subject matter

    C. must not know only her subject matter

    D. No change is necessary

Answer: D. No change is necessary
Options A, B, and C incorrectly use the correlative conjunction "not only." The "not only" must come directly after "know" in order to create the clearest meaning link with the "but also" predicate section later in the sentence.

Mathematics Posttest

1. **Express .0000456 in scientific notation.**
   (Easy) (Skill 5.1)

   A. 4.56×10^{-4}

   B. 45.6×10^{-6}

   C. 4.56×10^{-6}

   D. 4.56×10^{-5}

2. **Change $.\overline{63}$ into a fraction in simplest form.**
   (Rigorous) (Skill 5.1)

   A. 63/100

   B. 7/11

   C. 6 3/10

   D. 2/3

3. **The digit 4 in the number 302.41 is in the:**
   (Easy) (Skill 5.1)

   A. Tenths place

   B. Ones place

   C. Hundredths place

   D. Hundreds place

4. **Which of the following illustrates an inverse property?**
   (Easy) (Skill 5.3)

   A. $a + b = a - b$

   B. $a + b = b + a$

   C. $a + 0 = a$

   D. $a + (-a) = 0$

5. **$7t - 4 \cdot 2t + 3t \cdot 4 \div 2 =$**
   (Average) (Skill 5.4)

   A. $5t$

   B. 0

   C. $31t$

   D. 18

6. **If cleaning costs are $32 for 4 hours, how much is it for 10.5 hours?**
   (Average) (Skill 5.2)

   A. $112.50

   B. $87

   C. $84

   D. $76.50

7. Estimate the sum of 1,498 + 1,309.
   (Easy) (Skill 5.1)

   A. 2,900

   B. 2,850

   C. 2,800

   D. 2,600

8. Mr. Brown feeds his cat premium cat food, which costs $40 per month. Approximately how much will it cost to feed her for one year?
   (Average) (Skill 5.2)

   A. $500

   B. $400

   C. $80

   D. $4,800

9. A carton of milk priced at $6.00 is 30% off. Another carton priced at $5.80 is 20% off. Which one is the better buy?
   (Rigorous) (Skill 5.2)

   A. The $5.80 carton

   B. The $6.00 carton

   C. Both are equal

   D. There is not enough information

10. What is 30% of 450?
    (Easy) (Skill 5.2)

    A. 120

    B. 135

    C. 115

    D. None of the above

11. Joe reads 20 words per minute, and Jan reads 80 words per minute. How many minutes will it take Joe to read the same number of words that it takes Jan 40 minutes to read?
    (Rigorous) (Skill 5.2)

    A. 10

    B. 20

    C. 80

    D. 160

12. An architect is constructing a model of a building by using a ratio of 1:300. If the height of the scale model is 3 1/2 inches, what is the height, in yards, of the actual building?
    (Easy) (Skill 6.3)

    A. 87

    B. 58 1/3

    C. 43 1/2

    D. 29 1/6

13. In the *xy*-coordinate plane, points (1, 2) and (*w*, 6) lie on a line whose slope is 1/2. What is the value of *w*?
    (Average) (Skill 7.3)

    A. 4

    B. 6

    C. 7

    D. 9

14. Solve for *x*:

    $3x + 5 \geq 8 + 7x$

    (Average) (Skill 8.3)

    A. $x \geq -\frac{3}{4}$

    B. $x \leq -\frac{3}{4}$

    C. $x \geq \frac{3}{4}$

    D. $x \leq \frac{3}{4}$

15. Solve for *x*:

    $7 + 3x - 6 = 3x + 5 - x$

    (Average) (Skill 8.3)

    A. 2.5

    B. 4

    C. 4.5

    D. 27

16. Marvin bought a bag of candy. He gave half of the pieces to his friend Mike and one-third of the pieces to his sister Lisa. He ate half of the remaining pieces and had 15 left. How many pieces of candy were in the bag in the beginning?
    (Rigorous) (Skill 8.3)

    A. 120

    B. 90

    C. 30

    D. 180

17. A boat travels 30 miles upstream in three hours. It makes the return trip in one and a half hours. What is the speed of the boat in still water? *(Rigorous) (Skill 8.3)*

    A. 10 mph

    B. 15 mph

    C. 20 mph

    D. 30 mph

18. What is the next term in the following sequence?

    $\dfrac{2}{7}, \dfrac{13}{21}, \dfrac{20}{21}, \dfrac{9}{7}, \ldots$

    (Rigorous) (Skill 8.1)

    A. $\dfrac{29}{21}$

    B. $\dfrac{17}{21}$

    C. $\dfrac{11}{7}$

    D. $\dfrac{34}{21}$

19. What is the tenth term in the following sequence?

    3, 6, 12, 24…

    (Rigorous) (Skill 8.1)

    A. 3,072

    B. 1,024

    C. 512

    D. 1,536

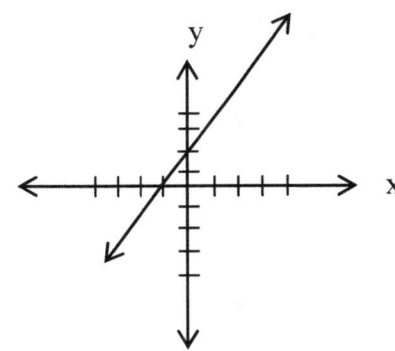

20. What is the equation of the graph above?
    (Average) (Skill 8.3)

    A. $2x + y = 2$

    B. $2x - y = -2$

    C. $2x - y = 2$

    D. $2x + y = -2$

21. The figure below represents the position (*x*), velocity (*v*), and acceleration (*a*) of a car moving in one direction as functions of time (*t*). According to the graph:

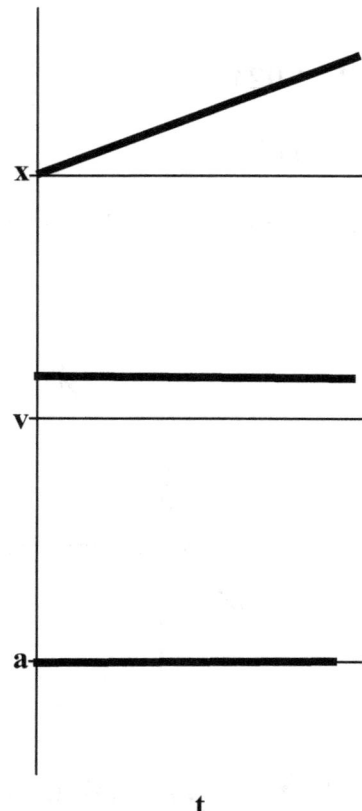

(Average) (Skill 9.1)

A. The car is at rest

B. The car is moving at a fixed speed

C. The car is speeding up

D. The car changes direction in the middle

22. Which of the following shapes is a rhombus?
    (Easy) (Skill 7.1)

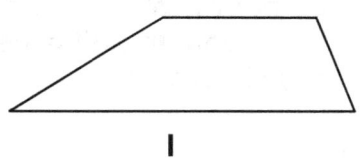

I

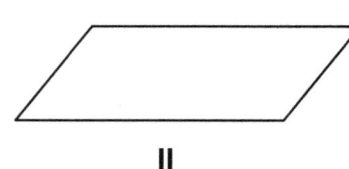

II

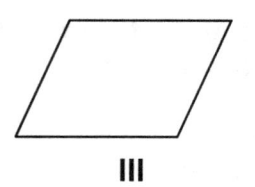

III

A. III

B. II

C. I

D. None of the above

23. The angles in any triangle:
    (Easy) (Skill 7.1)

A. Add up to 180 degrees

B. Are all equal

C. Are all right angles

D. Add up to 90 degrees

24. If a ship sails due south 6 miles, then due west 8 miles, how far is it from the starting point?
    (Average) (Skill 7.2)

    A. 100 miles

    B. 10 miles

    C. 14 miles

    D. 48 miles

25. A car is driven north at 74 miles per hour from point A. Another car is driven due east at 65 miles per hour starting from the same point at the same time. How far away from each other are the cars after 2 hours?
    (Rigorous) (Skill 7.2)

    A. 175.87 miles

    B. 232.66 miles

    C. 196.99 miles

    D. 202.43 miles

26. The mass of a cookie is closest to:
    (Average) (Skill 6.4)

    A. 0.5 kilogram

    B. 0.5 gram

    C. 15 grams

    D. 1.5 grams

27. You have a gallon of water and remove a total of 30 ounces. How many milliliters do you have left?
    (Rigorous) (Skill 6.4)

    A. 2,900 ml

    B. 1,100 ml

    C. 980 ml

    D. 1,000 ml

28. Seventh grade students are working on a project using nonstandard measurement. Which would *not* be an appropriate instrument for measuring the length of the classroom?
    (Average) (Skill 6.4)

    A. A student's foot

    B. A student's arm span

    C. A student's jump

    D. All are appropriate

29.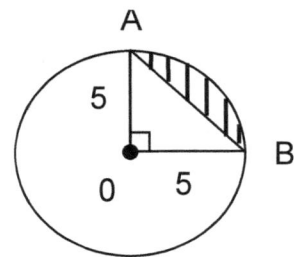

Compute the area of the shaded region, given a radius of 5 meters. *O* is the center.
(Rigorous) (Skill 6.1)

A. 7.13 cm²

B. 7.13 m²

C. 78.5 m²

D. 19.63 m²

30. Find the area of the figure pictured below.

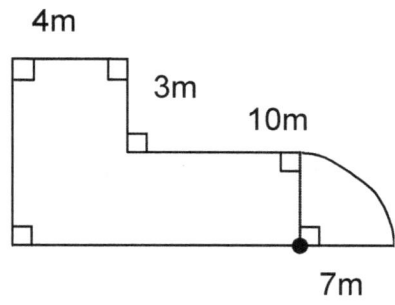

(Rigorous) (Skill 6.1)

A. 136.47 m²

B. 148.48 m²

C. 293.86 m²

D. 178.47 m²

31. Using a stopwatch, which of the following would be a more precise reading than 8 minutes, 57 seconds?
(Average) (Skill 6.6)

A. 08:57

B. 08

C. 08:57:03

D. 08:57:00

32. A school band has 200 members. Looking at the pie chart below, determine which statement is true about the band.

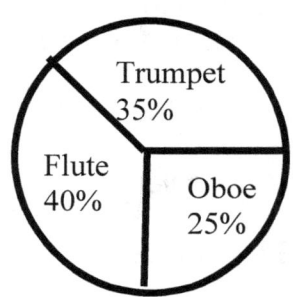

(Average) (Skill 9.1)

A. There are more trumpet players than flute players

B. There are fifty oboe players in the band

C. There are forty flute players in the band

D. One-third of all band members play the trumpet

33. You wish to create a visual display showing test score trends over several decades for a school. What kind of chart would be the most suitable? *(Average) (Skill 9.1)*

    A. Circle graph

    B. Bar graph

    C. Histogram

    D. Line graph

34. Which of the following statements is *not* true about the graph shown below? *(Average) (Skill 9.1*

    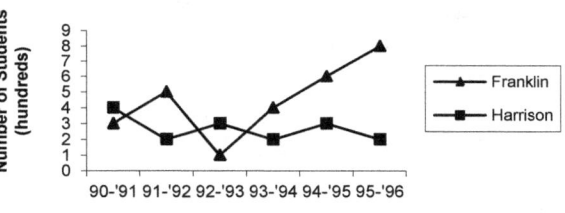

    A. Franklin school shows a rising trend in student enrollment

    B. Harrison school shows a falling trend in student enrollment

    C. Both schools show similar trends in student enrollment

    D. Neither school has had more than 900 students

35. The stem and leaf plot below shows the heights of several children in a class in feet. What is the median height? *(Average) (Skill 9.3)*

3	6 9
4	1 2 3 4 4 9
5	1 3 5

    A. 4 ft.

    B. 4.9 ft.

    C. 4.4 ft.

    D. 5.1 ft.

36. Which of these statements about the following data set is correct?

    {2, 5, 12, 6, 3, 9, 5, 12, 20, 2, 3, 5, 21, 12}

    (Rigorous) (Skill 9.3)

    A. There are 2 modes, the median is 8.5, and the range is 10

    B. There are 2 modes, the median is 5.5, and the range is 19

    C. There are 4 modes, the median is 5.5, and the range is 19

    D. There are 2 modes, the median is 5.5, and the range is 10

37. Compute the median for the following data set:

    {12, 19, 13, 16, 17, 14}

    (Average) (Skill 9.3)

    A. 14.5

    B. 15.17

    C. 15

    D. 16

38. How many ways are there to choose a potato and two green vegetables from a choice of three potatoes and seven green vegetables?
    (Rigorous) (Skill 9.6)

    A. 126

    B. 63

    C. 21

    D. 252

39. How many three-letter sequences can be formed if the first letter must always be a consonant (not *a, e, i, o, u*), the second letter must always be a vowel (*a, e, i, o,* or *u*), and the third letter must be different from the first?
    (Rigorous) (Skill 9.6)

    A. 2,100

    B. 4,056

    C. 3,250

    D. 2,625

40. Given a spinner with the numbers 1 through 8, what is the probability that you will not spin an even number or a number greater than 4?
    (Rigorous) (Skill 9.5)

    A. ¼

    B. ½

    C. ¾

    D. 1

41. Find the LCM of 27, 90, and 84.
    (Rigorous) (Skill 5.3)

    A. 90

    B. 3,780

    C. 204,120

    D. 1,260

42. The following equation is the best choice for teaching use of the distributive law in solving equations:
    (Average) (Skill 8.2)

    A. $3(x + 5) = 4x$

    B. $x(3 + 5) = 4$

    C. $4(x + 2x) = 2$

    D. None of the above

43. Oliver has *m* pennies, *p* dimes, and *t* quarters. If his friend gives him five more quarters, how many cents will Oliver have?
    (Rigorous) (Skill 8.3)

    A. $m + p + t + 5$

    B. $m + p + 25t + 5$

    C. $m + 10p + 25(t + 5)$

    D. $m + 5 + 10p + 25t$

44. Find the surface area of a box that is 3 feet wide, 5 feet tall, and 4 feet deep.
    (Rigorous) (Skill 6.1)

    A. 47 sq. ft.

    B. 60 sq. ft.

    C. 94 sq. ft

    D. 188 sq. ft.

45. In the *xy*-coordinate plane, the endpoints of a particular line segment are (4, 1) and (10, 3). This segment will be moved four units to the right and six units down. What will be the new coordinates of the midpoint of this segment?
    (Rigorous) (Skill 7.4)

    A. (7, 2)

    B. (11, -4)

    C. (14, 4)

    D. (10, 2)

Answer Key: Mathematics Posttest

1.	D		24.	B
2.	B		25.	C
3.	A		26.	C
4.	D		27.	A
5.	A		28.	C
6.	C		29.	B
7.	C		30.	B
8.	A		31.	C
9.	B		32.	B
10.	B		33.	D
11.	D		34.	C
12.	D		35.	C
13.	D		36.	B
14.	B		37.	C
15.	B		38.	B
16.	D		39.	D
17.	B		40.	A
18.	D		41.	B
19.	D		42.	A
20.	B		43.	C
21.	B		44.	C
22.	A		45.	B
23.	A			

Rigor Table: Mathematics Posttest

Rigor Level	Easy 18%	Average 40%	Rigorous 42%
Questions	1, 3, 4, 7, 10, 12, 22, 23	5, 6, 8, 13, 14, 15, 20, 21, 24, 26, 28, 31, 32, 33, 34, 35, 37, 42	2, 9, 11, 16, 17, 18, 19, 25, 27, 29, 30, 36, 38, 39, 40, 41, 43, 44, 45

Posttest with Rationales: Mathematics

1. **Express .0000456 in scientific notation.**
   (Easy) (Skill 5.1)

    A. 4.56×10^{-4}

    B. 45.6×10^{-6}

    C. 4.56×10^{-6}

    D. 4.56×10^{-5}

Answer: D. 4.56×10^{-5}
In scientific notation, the decimal point belongs to the right of the 4, the first significant digit. To get from 4.56×10^{-5} back to 0.0000456, we would move the decimal point 5 places to the left.

2. **Change $.\overline{63}$ into a fraction in simplest form.**
   (Rigorous) (Skill 5.1)

    A.   6 3/100

    B.   7/11

    C.   6 3/10

    D.   2/3

Answer: B. 7/11
Let $N = .636363\ldots$. Then, multiplying both sides of the equation by 100 or 10^2 (because there are two repeated numbers), we get $100N = 63.636363\ldots$ Then subtracting the two equations ($N = .636363\ldots$ and $100N = 63.636363\ldots$), gives $99N = 63$ or $N = \dfrac{63}{99} = \dfrac{7}{11}$.

3. The digit 4 in the number 302.41 is in the:
   (Easy) (Skill 5.1)

   A.   Tenths place

   B.   Ones place

   C.   Hundredths place

   D.   Hundreds place

Answer: A. Tenths place
The digit 4 is in the tenths place; the digit 1 is in the hundredths place.

4. Which of the following illustrates an inverse property?
   (Easy) (Skill 5.3)

   A. $a + b = a - b$

   B. $a + b = b + a$

   C. $a + 0 = a$

   D. $a + (-a) = 0$

Answer: D. $a + (-a) = 0$
The equation $a + (-a) = 0$ is a statement of the additive inverse property of algebra.

5. $7t - 4 \cdot 2t + 3t \cdot 4 \div 2 =$
   (Average) (Skill 5.4)

   A. $5t$

   B.   0

   C. $31t$

   D. $18t$

Answer: A. $5t$
Using the order of operations, first perform multiplication and division from left to right, $7t - 8t + 6t$, then add and subtract from left to right.

161

6. **If cleaning costs are $32 for 4 hours, how much is it for 10.5 hours?**
   (Average) (Skill 5.2)

   A. $112.50

   B. $87

   C. $84

   D. $76.50

Answer: C. $84
The hourly rate is $8 per hour, so 8 x 10.5 = $84.

7. **Estimate the sum of 1,498 + 1,309.**
   (Easy) (Skill 5.1)

   A.   2,900

   B.   2,850

   C.   2,800

   D.   2,600

Answer: C. 2,800
As this is an estimate, you add 1,500 and 1,300 to get 2,800.

8. **Mr. Brown feeds his cat premium cat food, which costs $40 per month. Approximately how much will it cost to feed her for one year?**
   (Average) (Skill 5.2)

   A. $500

   B. $400

   C. $80

   D. $4,800

Answer: A. $500
12 x 40 = 480, which is closest to $500.

9. **A carton of milk priced at $6.00 is 30% off. Another carton priced at $5.80 is 20% off. Which one is the better buy?**
   (Rigorous) (Skill 5.2)

   A.   The $5.80 carton

   B.   The $6.00 carton

   C.   Both are equal

   D.   There is not enough information

Answer: B. The $6.00 carton
The sale price of the $6.00 carton = $6.00 \times 0.7 = \$4.20$; the sale price of the $5.80 carton = $5.80 \times 0.8 = \$4.64$. Hence, the $6.00 carton is the better buy.

10. **What is 30% of 450?**
    (Easy) (Skill 5.2)

    A.   120

    B.   135

    C.   115

    D.   None of the above

Answer: B. 135
The percentage is given by $\frac{30}{100} \times 450 = 135$.

11. Joe reads 20 words per minute, and Jan reads 80 words per minute. How many minutes will it take Joe to read the same number of words that it takes Jan 40 minutes to read?
   (Rigorous) (Skill 5.2)

   A.   10

   B.   20

   C.   80

   D.   160

Answer: D. 160
If Jan reads 80 words per minute, she will read 3,200 words in 40 minutes. Assume that Joe reads 3,200 words in x minutes and set up a proportion relationship:

$$\frac{20}{1} = \frac{3200}{x}$$

Cross-multiplying, $20x = 3{,}200$; $x = 3{,}200/20 = 160$.

12. An architect is constructing a model of a building by using a ratio of 1:300. If the height of the scale model is 3 1/2 inches, what is the height, in yards, of the actual building?
   (Easy) (Skill 6.3)

   A.   87

   B.   58 1/3

   C.   43 1/2

   D.   29 1/6

Answer: D. 29 1/6
The height of the actual building, in inches, is 300 x 3 1/2 = 1,050. Since 36 inches is equivalent to 1 yard, a height of 1,050 inches is equivalent to 1,050/36 = 29 1/6 yards.

13. In the *xy*-coordinate plane, points (1, 2) and (*w*, 6) lie on a line whose slope is 1/2. What is the value of *w*?
    (Average) (Skill 7.3)

    A. 4

    B. 6

    C. 7

    D. 9

Answer: D. 9
Using the given points, the slope of this line can be written as $(6 - 2)/(w - 1) = 4/(w - 1)$. Then $4/(w - 1) = 1/2$. Cross-multiply to get $(w - 1) \times 1 = 4 \times 2$, which simplifies to $w - 1 = 8$. Thus, $w = 9$.

14. Solve for *x:*

    $3x + 5 \geq 8 + 7x$

    (Average) (Skill 8.3)

    A. $x \geq -\frac{3}{4}$

    B. $x \leq -\frac{3}{4}$

    C. $x \geq \frac{3}{4}$

    D. $x \leq \frac{3}{4}$

Answer: B. $x \leq -\frac{3}{4}$
Using additive equality, $-3 \geq 4x$. Divide both sides by 4 to obtain $-3/4 \geq x$.

15. Solve for *x*:

    $7 + 3x - 6 = 3x + 5 - x$

    (Average) (Skill 8.3)

    A.   2.5

    B.   4

    C.   4.5

    D.   27

Answer: B. 4
$7 + 3x - 6 = 3x + 5 - x$; $7 - 6 = 5 - x$; $-x = 1 - 5 = -4$; $x = 4$.

16. Marvin bought a bag of candy. He gave half of the pieces to his friend Mike and one-third of the pieces to his sister Lisa. He ate half of the remaining pieces and had 15 left. How many pieces of candy were in the bag in the beginning?
    (Rigorous) (Skill 8.3)

    A.   120

    B.   90

    C.   30

    D.   180

Answer: D. 180
Let the original number of pieces of candy in the bag be *x*. Mike got *x*/2 pieces of candy and Lisa got *x*/3 pieces. The number of pieces left =

$$x - \frac{x}{2} - \frac{x}{3} = \frac{6x}{6} - \frac{3x}{6} - \frac{2x}{6} = \frac{x}{6}$$

After Marvin ate half the remaining pieces *x*/12 pieces were left. Since *x*/12 = 15, the original number of pieces *x* = 12 × 15 = 180.

17. A boat travels 30 miles upstream in three hours. It makes the return trip in one and a half hours. What is the speed of the boat in still water? *(Rigorous) (Skill 8.3)*

    A.   10 mph

    B.   15 mph

    C.   20 mph

    D.   30 mph

Answer: B. 15 mph
Let x = the speed of the boat in still water and c = the speed of the current.

	rate	time	distance
upstream	$x - c$	3	30
downstream	$x + c$	1.5	30

Solve the system:
$$3x - 3c = 30$$
$$1.5x + 1.5c = 30$$

Multiply the 2nd equation by 2, $3x + 3c = 60$; add the two equations, $6x = 90$; and solve for x.

$x = 90/6 = 15$.

18. What is the next term in the following sequence?

$$\frac{2}{7}, \frac{13}{21}, \frac{20}{21}, \frac{9}{7}, \ldots$$

(Rigorous) (Skill 8.1)

A. $\frac{29}{21}$

B. $\frac{17}{21}$

C. $\frac{11}{7}$

D. $\frac{34}{21}$

Answer: D. $\frac{34}{21}$

This is an arithmetic sequence where each term is obtained by adding the common difference 7/21 or 1/3 to the preceding term. Thus the next term in the sequence is 9/7 + 1/3 = 34/21.

19. What is the tenth term in the following sequence?

3, 6, 12, 24…

(Rigorous) (Skill 8.1)

A. 3,072

B. 1,024

C. 512

D. 1,536

Answer: D. 1,536

This is a geometric sequence where each term is obtained by multiplying the previous term by 2. Hence the tenth term = 3×2^9 = 1,536.

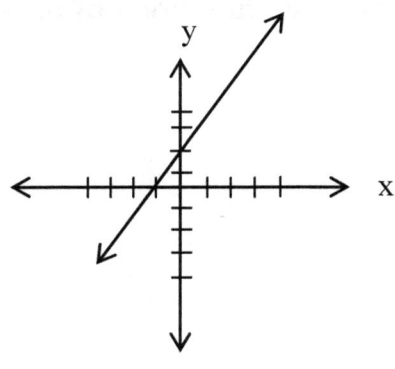

20. What is the equation of the graph above?
(Average) (Skill 8.3)

A. $2x + y = 2$

B. $2x - y = -2$

C. $2x - y = 2$

D. $2x + y = -2$

Answer: B. $2x - y = -2$

By observation, we see that the graph has a *y*-intercept of 2 and a slope of 2/1 = 2. Therefore, the graph's equation is *y* = *mx* + *b* = 2*x* + 2. Rearranging the terms gives 2*x* – *y* = -2.

21. The figure below represents the position (*x*), velocity (*v*), and acceleration (*a*) of a car moving in one direction as functions of time (*t*). According to the graph:

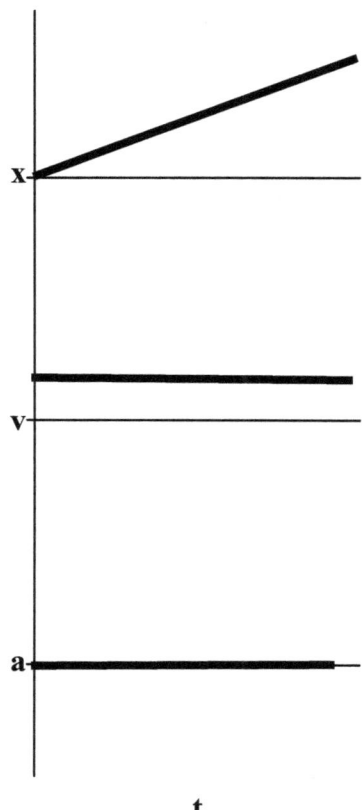

(Average) (Skill 9.1)

A. The car is at rest

B. The car is moving at a fixed speed

C. The car is speeding up

D. The car changes direction in the middle

Answer: B. The car is moving at a fixed speed
Since the acceleration is zero, the velocity is constant and nonzero, and the position is changing, the car is moving at a fixed speed.

22. Which of the following shapes is a rhombus?
(Easy) (Skill 7.1)

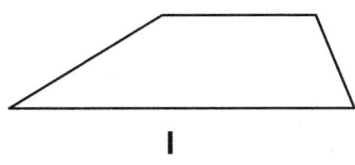

I

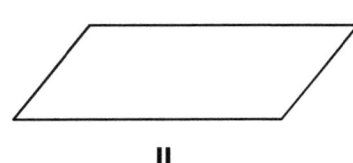

II

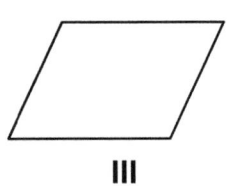

III

A. III

B. II

C. I

D. None of the above

Answer: A. III
A rhombus is a parallelogram with four equal sides.

23. The angles in any triangle:
   (Easy) (Skill 7.1)

   A. Add up to 180 degrees

   B. Are all equal

   C. Are all right angles

   D. Add up to 90 degrees

Answer: A. Add up to 180 degrees
The angles of a triangle, when totaled, equal 180 degrees.

24. If a ship sails due south 6 miles, then due west 8 miles, how far is it from the starting point?
(Average) (Skill 7.2)

   A. 100 miles

   B. 10 miles

   C. 14 miles

   D. 48 miles

Answer: B. 10 miles
Draw a right triangle with legs of 6 and 8. Then, find the hypotenuse using the Pythagorean Theorem: $6^2 + 8^2 = c^2$. Therefore, $c = 10$ miles.

25. A car is driven north at 74 miles per hour from point A. Another car is driven due east at 65 miles per hour starting from the same point at the same time. How far away from each other are the cars after 2 hours?
(Rigorous) (Skill 7.2)

   A.   175.87 miles

   B.   232.66 miles

   C.   196.99 miles

   D.   202.43 miles

Answer: C. 196.99 miles
The routes the cars take form a right triangle with edges 74 x 2 and 65 x 2. This gives two sides of a right triangle of 148 and 130. Using the Pythagorean Theorem, we get $148^2 + 130^2 = $ distance^2. Therefore, the distance between the cars is 196.99 miles.

26. The mass of a cookie is closest to:
(Average) (Skill 6.4)

   A.   0.5 kilogram

   B.   0.5 gram

   C.   15 grams

   D.   1.5 grams

Answer: C. 15 grams
In terms of commonly used U.S. units, 15 grams is about half an ounce and 0.5 kilogram is about a pound.

27. You have a gallon of water and remove a total of 30 ounces. How many milliliters do you have left?
   (Rigorous) (Skill 6.4)

   A.   2,900 ml

   B.   1,100 ml

   C.   980 ml

   D.   1,000 ml

Answer: A. 2,900 ml
1 gallon = 128 fluid ounces. If 30 ounces are removed, you have 98 ounces left. Since 1 fluid ounce = 29.6 ml, 98 ounces = 2,900 ml.

28. Seventh grade students are working on a project using nonstandard measurement. Which would *not* be an appropriate instrument for measuring the length of the classroom?
   (Average) (Skill 6.4)

   A.   A student's foot

   B.   A student's arm span

   C.   A student's jump

   D.   All are appropriate

Answer: C. A student's jump
Whereas a student's foot or student's arm span has a fixed length, a student's jump can vary in length and would therefore not be an appropriate unit.

29.

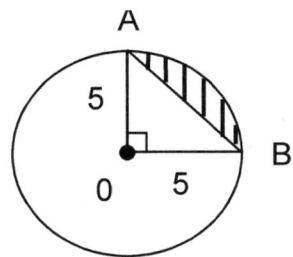

Compute the area of the shaded region, given a radius of 5 meters. O is the center.
(Rigorous) (Skill 6.1)

A.   7.13 cm²

B.   7.13 m²

C.   78.5 m²

D.   19.63 m²

Answer: B. 7.13 m²

The area of triangle *AOB* is .5(5)(5) = 12.5 square meters. Since $\frac{90}{360} = .25$, the area of sector *AOB* (pie-shaped piece) is approximately $.25(\pi)5^2 = 19.63$. Subtracting the triangle area from the sector area to get the area of the shaded region, we get approximately 19.63 - 12.5 = 7.13 square meters.

30. Find the area of the figure pictured below.

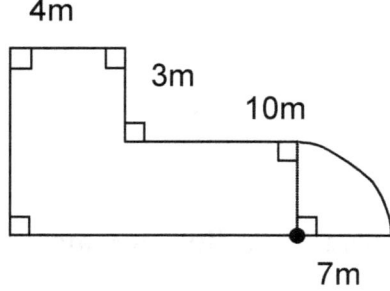

(Rigorous) (Skill 6.1)

A. 136.47 m²

B. 148.48 m²

C. 293.86 m²

D. 178.47 m²

Answer: B. 148.48 m²

Divide the figure into two rectangles and one quarter circle. The tall rectangle on the left will have dimensions 10 by 4 and an area of 40. The rectangle in the center will have dimensions 7 by 10 and an area of 70. The quarter circle will have area $.25(\pi)7^2 = 38.48$. The total area is therefore approximately 148.48 square meters.

31. Using a stopwatch, which of the following would be a more precise reading than 8 minutes, 57 seconds?
(Average) (Skill 6.6)

   A.   08:57

   B.   08

   C.   08:57:03

   D.   08:57:00

Answer: C. 08:57:03
Only Option C gives a correct and more precise reading: 8 minutes, 57 seconds, and three hundredths of a second. Stopwatches allow more precise measurement of time than a clock or wristwatch can, by providing units smaller than a second.

32. A school band has 200 members. Looking at the pie chart below, determine which statement is true about the band.

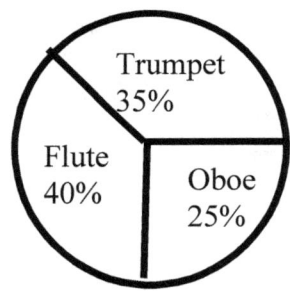

(Average) (Skill 9.1)

   A.   There are more trumpet players than flute players

   B.   There are fifty oboe players in the band

   C.   There are forty flute players in the band

   D.   One-third of all band members play the trumpet

Answer: B. There are fifty oboe players in the band
The band has 200 members, and 25% of 200 is 50.

33. You wish to create a visual display showing test score trends over several decades for a school. What kind of chart would be the most suitable?
(Average) (Skill 9.1)

   A.   Circle graph

   B.   Bar graph

   C.   Histogram

   D.   Line graph

Answer: D. Line graph
A line graph with the years plotted along the horizontal axis would be the best visual display of trends.

34. Which of the following statements is *not* true about the graph shown below?
(Average) (Skill 9.1)

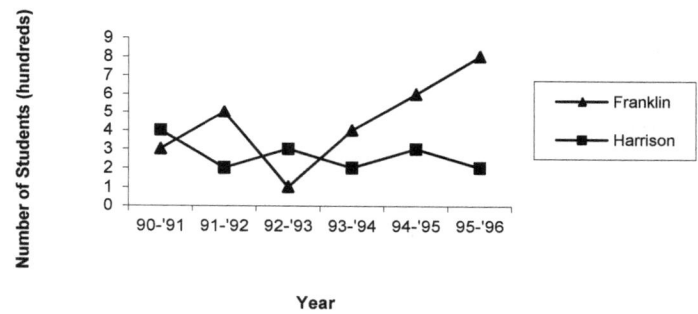

   A.   Franklin school shows a rising trend in student enrollment

   B.   Harrison school shows a falling trend in student enrollment

   C.   Both schools show similar trends in student enrollment

   D.   Neither school has had more than 900 students

Answer: C. Both schools show similar trends in student enrollment
The two schools show different enrollment trends.

35. The stem and leaf plot below shows the heights of several children in a class in feet. What is the median height?
(Average) (Skill 9.3)

3	6 9
4	1 2 3 4 4 9
5	1 3 5

A. 4 ft.

B. 4.9 ft.

C. 4.4 ft.

D. 5.1 ft.

Answer: C. 4.4 ft.
In the stem and leaf plot, the feet are listed in the first column and inches in the second column. To calculate the median, arrange the heights in ascending order: 3.6, 3.9, 4.1, 4.2, 4.3, 4.4, 4.4, 4.9, 5.1, 5.3, 5.5. The height of 4.4 feet is in the center of this list.

36. Which of these statements about the following data set is correct?

{2, 5, 12, 6, 3, 9, 5, 12, 20, 2, 3, 5, 21, 12}

(Rigorous) (Skill 9.3)

A. There are 2 modes, the median is 8.5, and the range is 10

B. There are 2 modes, the median is 5.5, and the range is 19

C. There are 4 modes, the median is 5.5, and the range is 19

D. There are 2 modes, the median is 5.5, and the range is 10

Answer: B. There are 2 modes, the median is 5.5, and the range is 19
The two modes are 5 and 12, since they each occur three times.

37. Compute the median for the following data set:

{12, 19, 13, 16, 17, 14}

(Average) (Skill 9.3)

    A.   14.5

    B.   15.17

    C.   15

    D.   16

Answer: C. 15
Arrange the data in ascending order: 12,13,14,16,17,19. The median is the middle value in a list with an odd number of entries. When there is an even number of entries, the median is the mean of the two center entries. Here the average of 14 and 16 is 15.

38. How many ways are there to choose a potato and two green vegetables from a choice of three potatoes and seven green vegetables? *(Rigorous) (Skill 9.6)*

    A.   126

    B.   63

    C.   21

    D.   252

Answer: B. 63
There are three ways to choose a potato and the number of ways to choose two green vegetables from seven is given by $\frac{7!}{5!2!} = 21$. Hence the total number of choices = 3 x 21 = 63.

39. How many three-letter sequences can be formed if the first letter must always be a consonant (not *a, e, i, o, u*), the second letter must always be a vowel (*a, e, i, o,* or *u*), and the third letter must be different from the first.
   (Rigorous) (Skill 9.6)

   A.   2,100

   B.   4,056

   C.   3,250

   D.   2,625

Answer: D. 2,625
There are 21 choices for the first letter, 5 choices for the second letter, and 25 choices for the third letter. Hence, the number of possible sequences = 21 x 5 x 25 = 2,625.

40. Given a spinner with the numbers 1 through 8, what is the probability that you will not spin an even number or a number greater than 4?
   (Rigorous) (Skill 9.5)

   A.   ¼

   B.   ½

   C.   ¾

   D.   1

Answer: A. ¼
There are eight possible outcomes. Of those, there are four even numbers 2, 4, 6, 8 and two other numbers (5 and 6) that are greater than 4. So six of the outcomes are even numbers or numbers greater than 4. Hence, there are just two outcomes (1 and 3) that are neither even nor greater than 4. Thus, the probability that you will not spin an even number or a number greater than 4 is 2 out of 8, i.e. ¼.

41. Find the LCM of 27, 90, and 84.
   (Rigorous) (Skill 5.3)

   A.   90

   B.   3,780

   C.   204,120

   D.   1,260

Answer: B. 3,780
To find the LCM of the three numbers, factor each into its prime factors and multiply each common factor the maximum number of times it occurs. Thus 27=3x3x3; 90=2x3x3x5; 84=2x2x3x7; LCM = 2x2x3x3x3x5x7=3,780.

42. The following equation is the best choice for teaching use of the distributive law in solving equations:
   (Average) (Skill 8.2)

   A. $3(x + 5) = 4x$

   B. $x(3 + 5) = 4$

   C. $4(x + 2x) = 2$

   D.   None of the above

Answer: A. $3(x + 5) = 4x$
One can apply the distributive law to Option B, but it is simpler to just add 3 and 5 and then multiply by x. One can also apply the distributive law to Option C, but the simpler option is to add x and $2x$ first and then multiply by 4. To solve Option A, one would have to apply the distributive law $3(x + 5) = 3x + 15$. Hence, A is the best choice.

43. Oliver has m pennies, p dimes, and t quarters. If his friend gives him five more quarters, how many cents will Oliver have?
(Rigorous) (Skill 8.3)

A. $m + p + t + 5$

B. $m + p + 25t + 5$

C. $m + 10p + 25(t + 5)$

D. $m + 5 + 10p + 25t$

Answer C. $m + 10p + 25(t + 5)$
The value of *m* pennies is *m* cents, the value of *p* dimes is 10*p* cents, and the value of *t* quarters is 25*t* cents. Before Oliver's friend gave him five quarters, Oliver had a total of $m + 10p + 25t$ cents. After receiving the additional five quarters, Oliver has an additional 25 x 5 cents. His total becomes $m + 10p + 25t + (25 \times 5)$, which is equivalent to $m + 10p + 25(t + 5)$ cents.

44. Find the surface area of a box that is 3 feet wide, 5 feet tall, and 4 feet deep.
(Rigorous) (Skill 6.1)

A. 47 sq. ft.

B. 60 sq. ft.

C. 94 sq. ft.

D. 188 sq. ft.

Answer: C. 94 sq. ft.
Let's assume the base of the rectangular solid (box) is 3 by 4, and the height is 5. Then the surface area of the top and bottom together is 2 x 12 = 24. The sum of the areas of the front and back is 2 x 15 = 30, while the sum of the areas of the sides are 2 x 20 = 40. The total surface area is therefore 94 square feet.

45. In the xy-coordinate plane, the endpoints of a particular line segment are (4, 1) and (10, 3). This segment will be moved four units to the right and six units down. What will be the new coordinates of the midpoint of this segment?
(Rigorous) (Skill 7.4)

   A. (7, 2)

   B. (11, -4)

   C. (14, 4)

   D. (10, 2)

Answer: B. (11, -4)
The midpoint of the line segment in its original location is ((4 + 10)/2, (1 + 3)/2) = (7, 2). After this segment is moved four units to the right and six units down, the location of the midpoint becomes (7 + 4, 2 – 6) = (11, -4).

Reading Posttest

DIRECTIONS: Read the following passage and answer the questions that follow.

Spiders can be found in almost all areas of the world with one exception, the polar regions, which are too cold for the spiders to exist. The habitats that most spiders live in, however, are the woodlands, grasslands, or forests where the insect population is high and allows spiders to catch them for food. Of course, spiders are also found in people's homes, but we don't often think about them because out of sight, out of mind, and spiders like to keep to themselves and often stay pretty well hidden. Surprisingly enough, some spiders even live on water! The water spider lives in slow moving or still water. Another water spider—the raft spider—lives in marshy places and can actually run across the surface of the water.

1. **What is the main idea of the passage?**
   (Average) (Skill 10.1)

   A. Each type of spider has a certain quality or characteristic

   B. Spiders live in many different areas around the world

   C. It is difficult to find spiders because they like to keep to themselves

   D. One type of spider is known as the raft spider and can run across water

2. **Why did the author write this article?**
   (Average) (Skill 11.1)

   A. To entertain

   B. To persuade

   C. To describe

   D. To inform

3. **What is the best summary of this paragraph?**
   (Rigorous) (Skill 10.2)

   A. Spiders reside in various habitats except for areas of extreme cold. They can even be found on water

   B. Spiders live in areas where the insect population is high so they can survive

   C. Spiders fit the saying, "out of sight, out of mind," because they are very private insects

   D. Spiders that run across the water are also known as raft spiders

4. **How is the passage organized?**
   (Average) (Skill 11.2)

   A. Sequence of events

   B. Compare and contrast

   C. Statement support

   D. Cause and effect

5. **What comparison is made in the paragraph?**
   (Rigorous) (Skill 11.6)

   A. Arctic spiders to woodland spiders

   B. People to spiders

   C. Woodland spiders to water spiders

   D. The arctic region to the woodland areas

6. **What is the author implying by using the words "surprisingly enough"?**
   (Rigorous) (Skill 10.1)

   A. She is scared of spiders that are able to live in the water

   B. She always thought that spiders were strictly land lubbers

   C. She thought they always stayed well-hidden, and water surfaces are not well-hidden

   D. She thinks that spiders are brought out into the water by rafts

7. **What words does the author use to clarify information for the reader?**
   (Average) (Skill 11.6)

   A. Actually

   B. Another water spider

   C. Raft spider

   D. Surprisingly enough

8. **What would have been the best transition word for the author to use to connect these two sentences?**
   (Easy) (Skill 10.1)

   Surprisingly enough, some spiders even live on water! The water spider lives in slow moving or still water.

   A. Then,

   B. Beyond,

   C. For example,

   D. Immediately,

9. **What does the word "meandered" mean in the sentence below?**
   (Easy) (Skill 10.3)

   Michael was taking a long time to return to his seat after sharpening his pencil at the back of the room. After leaving the sharpener, he meandered around the room before eventually making his way back to his own seat.

   A. rolled

   B. roamed

   C. slithered

   D. stomped

10. **What does the word "interject" mean in the sentence below?**
    (Easy) (Skill 10.3)

    Nancy was speaking with her best friend Sierra. Nancy's little sister was standing nearby and was eavesdropping on their conversation. Suddenly, she heard something that interested her and had to interject her opinion about the subject the girls were talking about.

    A. repeat

    B. pierce

    C. intersect

    D. state

11. When reading the book *Stormbreaker* by Anthony Horowitz, the reader feels like they are a part of the action. The author uses so many details to bring the reader into the setting of the story, and this puts the reader right beside Alex Rider, the main character in the story.

    Is this a valid or invalid argument?
    (Average) (Skill 11.7)

    A. Valid

    B. Invalid

12. Let's go see the movie *Alice in Wonderland*. It's a great movie and Johnny Depp is awesome!

    Is this a valid or invalid argument?
    (Average) (Skill 11.7)

    A. Valid

    B. Invalid

DIRECTIONS: Read the following passage and answer the questions that follow.

Mr. Smith gave instructions for the painting to be hung on the wall. And then it leaped forth before his eyes: the little cottages on the river, the white clouds floating over the valley, and the green of the towering mountain ranges that were seen in the distance. The painting was so vivid that it seemed almost real. Mr. Smith was now absolutely certain that the painting had been worth the money.

13. **Is this passage biased?**
    (Rigorous) (Skill 11.4)

    A. Yes

    B. No

14. **From the last sentence, one can infer that:**
    (Rigorous) (Skill 11.8)

    A. The painting was expensive.

    B. The painting was cheap.

    C. Mr. Smith was considering purchasing the painting.

    D. Mr. Smith thought the painting was too expensive and decided not to purchase it.

15. **Boys are smarter than girls. Is this sentence fact or opinion?**
    (Easy) (Skill 11.3)

    A. Fact

    B. Opinion

16. Turkey burgers are better than beef burgers. Is this sentence fact or opinion?
    (Easy) (Skill 11.3)

    A. Fact

    B. Opinion

17. Johnny Depp stars in the movie *Charlie and the Chocolate Factory*.

    Is this sentence fact or opinion?
    (Easy) (Skill 11.3)

    A. Fact

    B. Opinion

18. We live at 5310 Fair Oaks Drive in Chicago, Illinois.

    Is this sentence fact or opinion?

    (Easy) (Skill 11.3)

    A. Fact

    B. Opinion

19. What conclusion can be drawn from the passage below?
    (Rigorous) (Skill 11.8)

    When she walked into the room she gasped in disbelief as her hands rose to her face and her eyes bulged large. After she picked her jaw up off the floor, a huge smile spread across her face as her best friend came up and wrapped her arms around her and wished her a happy birthday.

    A. The girl didn't know anyone in the room

    B. The girl saw something shocking

    C. The girl was being thrown a surprise party

    D. The girl got punched in the face

20. **What conclusion can be drawn from the paragraph below?** *(Average) (Skill 11.8)*

   Joel stood at the water's edge staring into the waves as his legs trembled violently. His mind flashed back to last summer and his entire body joined his legs and began to tremble. He tried to even his breathing as he took slow deep breaths before deciding to head into the surf.

   A. The water was really cold

   B. Joel saw a shark in the water

   C. Last summer was better than this summer

   D. Joel is afraid of the water because something happened

DIRECTIONS: Read the following passage and answer the questions that follow.

Deciding which animal to get as the family pet can be a very difficult decision, and there are many things to take into consideration. First, you must consider the size of your home and the area that will be dedicated to the pet. If your home is a smaller one, then you probably want to get a small dog or even a cat. If you are lucky enough to have larger home with plenty of room inside and out, then most certainly consider a large or even a more active breed of dog. One other thing to consider is how often and how long you are outside of the home. Cats do not need to be let out to relieve themselves. They are normally trained to use a litter box. On the other hand, dogs require being let out. Dogs also require more exercise than cats and often need to be walked. This can be aggravating to an owner especially on rainy days. Therefore, when deciding which pet is best for your family, it is necessary to consider more than whether or not you want a dog or a cat, but which animal will best fit into your family's lifestyle.

21. **How does the author feel about dogs?**
    (Rigorous) (Skill 11.5)

    A. The author likes dogs and cats the same

    B. The author thinks that dogs are aggravating

    C. The author believes they require more care than cats

    D. The author feels that dogs are more active than cats

22. **How does the author feel about the size of people's houses?**
    (Rigorous) (Skill 11.5)

    A. The author believes that people with larger homes are lucky

    B. The author thinks that if you have a small house you should have a cat

    C. The author feels that only people with large homes should own animals

    D. The author thinks that only those who own homes should own pets

23. **From this passage, one can infer that:**
    (Rigorous) (Skill 11.8)

    A. The author owns a cat

    B. More people own dogs than cats

    C. Cats are smarter than dogs

    D. The author owns a dog

24. **From this passage, one can infer that:**
    (Rigorous) (Skill 11.8)

    A. Either a dog or cat will be right for every family who wants a pet

    B. Choosing a pet is not solely one family member's job

    C. Only someone who enjoys exercising should get a dog

    D. Big dogs will not survive in a small house

DIRECTIONS: Read the following passage and answer the questions that follow.

According to Factmonster.com, the most popular Internet activity is sending and/or reading email. Approximately 92% of Internet users report using the Internet for this purpose. 89% of Internet users report that they use the Internet to search for information. Two popular search engines are Google and Yahoo! The introduction of the Internet has made it easy to gather and research information quickly. Other reasons that Internet users use the Internet is to search for driving directions, look into a hobby or interest, or research a product or service before buying, just to name a few. Creative <u>enterprises</u> such as remixing songs or lyrics stood at the bottom of reasons people use the Internet. Surprisingly, only 11% of Internet users said they use the Internet for creative purposes. Perhaps people are using specific software to be creative. Where do you rank? Think about why you last used the Internet.

25. **What is the main idea of the passage?**
(Average) (Skill 10.1)

   A. Factmonster has a lot of great facts for people to research

   B. People use the Internet for a variety of reasons

   C. The main reason the Internet is used is to check emails

   D. People aren't as creative as they used to be before the Internet

26. **Why did the author write this article?**
(Average) (Skill 11.1)

   A. To convince the reader to use the Internet

   B. To teach the reader how use the Internet

   C. To encourage the reader to use the Internet

   D. To inform the reader about Internet usage trends

27. **How is the passage organized?**
(Average) (Skill 11.2)

   A. Sequence of events

   B. Cause and effect

   C. Statement support

   D. Compare and contrast

28. **What cause and effect relationship exists in this paragraph?**
    (Rigorous) (Skill 11.6)

    A. The U.S. postal service is suffering from the introduction of email

    B. Google and Yahoo! are used most often to search information

    C. The introduction of the Internet has made gathering information easy

    D. People are less creative since they aren't using their computers for this reason

29. **By using the word "surprisingly" in the passage, what is the author implying?**
    (Rigorous) (Skill 10.1)

    A. It is thought that the Internet is used more creative purposes

    B. People are thought to be more creative than they really are

    C. It is thought that fewer than 11% would use the Internet for creative purposes

    D. Software companies are making 11% more creative software

30. **Which transition word could the author have used to connect these two sentences?**
    (Average) (Skill 10.1)

    Approximately 92% of Internet users report using the Internet for this purpose. 89% of Internet users report that they use the Internet to search for information.

    A. Additionally,

    B. Therefore,

    C. Next,

    D. Similarly,

31. **What does the word "enterprises" mean in the passage?**
    (Average) (Skill 10.3)

    A. people

    B. endeavors

    C. businesses

    D. musicians

DIRECTIONS: Read the following passage and answer the questions that follow.

The poems both use personification to bring the subjects of the poem to life. Both poems were also very entertaining. In "The Subway" the author says that the subway, also known as a dragon, swallows up the people and then spits them out at the next stop. Similarly, in "Steam Shovel," the author says that the steam shovel chews up the dirt that it scoops up and smiles amiably at the people below.

The subjects of the poems are compared to different things. The subway is compared to a dragon with green scales. Dragons breathe fire. The steam shovel is compared to an ancient dinosaur with a long neck and dripping jaws.

32. **How is the passage organized?**
    (Average) (Skill 11.2)

    A. Compare and contrast

    B. Cause and effect

    C. Sequence of events

    D. Statement support

33. **Which sentence in the passage is irrelevant?**
    (Average) (Skill 11.6)

    A. Both poems were also very entertaining.

    B. The subway is also known as a dragon.

    C. The subway swallows people up and spits them out.

    D. The author says that the steam shovel chews up the dirt.

34. **Which sentence in the passage is irrelevant?**
    (Rigorous) (Skill 11.6)

    A. The subjects of the poems are compared to different things.

    B. The subway is compared to a dragon with green scales.

    C. Dragons breathe fire.

    D. The steam shovel is compared to an ancient dinosaur.

DIRECTIONS: Read the following passage and answer the questions that follow.

Have you ever wondered what chewing gum is made from? What is it that allows us to chew it for hours without it ever disintegrating? Chicle is a gum, or sap, that comes from the sapodilla tree. The sapodilla tree is an American tropical evergreen that is native to South Florida. Flavorings, corn syrup, and sugar or artificial sweeteners are other ingredients that go into the production of chewing gum. Legend has it that Native Americans chewed spruce resin to quench their thirst. Today, gum is chewed for many reasons by many different groups of people.

35. **What conclusion can be drawn from the passage?**
    (Rigorous) (Skill 11.8)

    A. Everyone in South Florida has heard of the sapodilla tree

    B. Many people have wondered what makes gum chewy

    C. Some type of sweetener is used in gum production

    D. Native Americans invented gum

36. **What can be inferred from the passage?**
    (Rigorous) (Skill 11.8)

    A. The gum Chiclets took its name from the ingredient chicle used in gum

    B. Gum is disgusting after it's been chewed for a few hours

    C. Gum is only made in the United States because that's where the sapodilla tree grows

    D. When someone is thirsty they should chew gum

DIRECTIONS: Read the following passage and answer the questions that follow.

The word "cycle" comes from the Greek word *kyklos*, which means "circle" or "wheel." There are many different types of cycles. The word "unicycle" comes from the prefix *uni-*, which means "one," combined with the root "cycle." When the prefix and root word cycle are combined, it creates a word that means "one circle or wheel." Unicycles are often used for entertainment rather than exercise.

    A prefix *bi-* means "two," which, when combined with the word "cycle," creates the word "bicycle." How many wheels does a bicycle have? Many young children ride a tricycle because it has three wheels and is easy to ride. The prefix *tri-* means "three," and when it is combined with the root word "cycle," the new word is "three wheels." It is even possible to make the word "motorcycle." Once you know how to use roots, it is easy to figure out the meaning of an unknown word.

37. **What is the main idea of the passage?**
 (Average) (Skill 10.1)

 A. There are many types of cycles

 B. The prefix *uni-* means "one"

 C. Words can be defined by their parts

 D. Unicycles are often used for entertainment

38. **What does the word "roots" mean in this passage?**
 (Easy) (Skill 10.3)

 A. Stable parts of plants

 B. Where one originated

 C. The base portions of a word

 D. A spelling tool

39. **Which is an opinion contained in this passage?**
 (Average) (Skill 11.3)

 A. Once you know how to use roots, it is easy to figure out the meaning of an unknown word

 B. Many young children ride a tricycle

 C. Unicycles are often used for entertainment rather than exercise

 D. The word "cycle" comes from the Greek word *kyklos*

40. From this article you can see that the author thinks:
(Rigorous) (Skill 11.5)

A. Riding a bicycle is good exercise

B. It is important to know about the English language

C. "Cycle" is a confusing word

D. It is more important to understand the prefixes and suffixes

Answer Key: Reading Posttest

1. B
2. D
3. A
4. C
5. D
6. B
7. C
8. C
9. B
10. D
11. A
12. B
13. B
14. A
15. B
16. B
17. A
18. A
19. C
20. D

21. C
22. A
23. D
24. B
25. B
26. D
27. C
28. C
29. A
30. A
31. B
32. A
33. A
34. C
35. C
36. A
37. C
38. C
39. A
40. B

Rigor Table: Reading Posttest

	Easy 20%	Average 40%	Rigorous 40%
Questions	8, 9, 10, 15, 16, 17, 18, 38	1, 2, 4, 7, 11, 12, 20, 25, 26, 27, 30, 31, 32, 33, 37, 39	3, 5, 6, 13, 14, 19, 21, 22, 23, 24, 28, 29, 34, 35, 36, 40

Posttest with Rationales: Reading

DIRECTIONS: Read the following passage and answer the questions that follow.

Spiders can be found in almost all areas of the world with one exception, the polar regions, which are too cold for the spiders to exist. The habitats that most spiders live in, however, are the woodlands, grasslands, or forests where the insect population is high and allows spiders to catch them for food. Of course, spiders are also found in people's homes, but we don't often think about them because out of sight, out of mind, and spiders like to keep to themselves and often stay pretty well hidden. Surprisingly enough, some spiders even live on water! The water spider lives in slow moving or still water. Another water spider—the raft spider—lives in marshy places and can actually run across the surface of the water.

1. **What is the main idea of the passage?**
   (Average) (Skill 10.1)

   A. Each type of spider has a certain quality or characteristic

   B. Spiders live in many different areas around the world

   C. It is difficult to find spiders because they like to keep to themselves

   D. One type of spider is known as the raft spider and can run across water

   Answer: B. Spiders live in many different areas around the world
   Options A, C, and D are all supporting details of the main idea, "Spiders live in many different areas around the world."

2. **Why did the author write this article?**
   (Average) (Skill 11.1)

   A.   To entertain

   B.   To persuade

   C.   To describe

   D.   To inform

Answer: D. To inform
The author wrote this article to teach its readers about the different types of spiders—in other words to inform them.

3. **What is the best summary of this paragraph?**
   (Rigorous) (Skill 10.2)

   A.   Spiders reside in various habitats except for areas of extreme cold. They can even be found on water

   B.   Spiders live in areas where the insect population is high so they can survive

   C.   Spiders fit the saying, "out of sight, out of mind," because they are very private insects

   D.   Spiders that run across the water are also known as raft spiders

Answer: A. Spiders reside in various habitats except for areas of extreme cold. They can even be found on water
Option A is the only choice that applies to the whole paragraph and is therefore the best summary.

4. **How is the passage organized?**
   (Average) (Skill 11.2)

   A. Sequence of events

   B. Compare and contrast

   C. Statement support

   D. Cause and effect

Answer: C. Statement support
The main idea of each paragraph is stated and then supporting sentences follow. Therefore, this is a "statement support" organization example.

5. **What comparison is made in the paragraph?**
   (Rigorous) (Skill 11.6)

   A. Arctic spiders to woodland spiders

   B. People to spiders

   C. Woodland spiders to water spiders

   D. The arctic region to the woodland areas

Answer: D. The arctic region to the woodland areas
The author begins the paragraph by comparing the arctic region to the woodland region and how they are different, and therefore, not appropriate for spiders to reside.

6. **What is the author implying by using the words "surprisingly enough"? (Rigorous) (Skill 10.1)**

    A.   She is scared of spiders that are able to live in the water

    B.   She always thought that spiders were strictly land lubbers

    C.   She thought they always stayed well-hidden, and water surfaces are not well-hidden

    D.   She thinks that spiders are brought out into the water by rafts

Answer: B. She always thought that spiders were strictly land lubbers
The author is implying that she is surprised that spiders can survive on the water because she thought they were strictly land creatures.

7. **What words does the author use to clarify information for the reader? (Average) (Skill 11.6)**

    A.   Actually

    B.   Another water spider

    C.   Raft spider

    D.   Surprisingly enough

Answer: C. Raft spider
By placing the words "raft spider" inside of dashes, the author is defining the name of the water spider mentioned in the sentence.

8. **What would have been the best transition word for the author to use to connect these two sentences?**
   (Easy) (Skill 10.1)

   Surprisingly enough, some spiders even live on water! The water spider lives in slow moving or still water.

   A. Then,

   B. Beyond,

   C. For example,

   D. Immediately,

Answer: C. For example,
"For example," would indicate that the author is going to offer an example as she has done in the paragraph. Therefore, it would have been the best transition word to use to connect the two sentences.

9. **What does the word "meandered" mean in the sentence below?**
   (Easy) (Skill 10.3)

   Michael was taking a long time to return to his seat after sharpening his pencil at the back of the room. After leaving the sharpener, he <u>meandered</u> around the room before eventually making his way back to his own seat.

   A. rolled

   B. roamed

   C. slithered

   D. stomped

Answer: B. roamed
The student *roamed* around the room before returning to his seat.

10. What does the word "interject" mean in the sentence below?
    (Easy) (Skill 10.3)

    Nancy was speaking with her best friend Sierra. Nancy's little sister was standing nearby and was eavesdropping on their conversation. Suddenly, she heard something that interested her and had to <u>interject</u> her opinion about the subject the girls were talking about.

    A. repeat

    B. pierce

    C. intersect

    D. state

Answer: D. state
By *interjecting* her opinion, Nancy's little sister had to "state" her opinion, or make her idea known.

11. When reading the book *Stormbreaker* by Anthony Horowitz, the reader feels like they are a part of the action. The author uses so many details to bring the reader into the setting of the story, and this puts the reader right beside Alex Rider, the main character in the story.

    Is this a valid or invalid argument?
    (Average) (Skill 11.7)

    A. Valid

    B. Invalid

Answer: A. Valid
The argument is valid because there is support that backs up the argument that while reading *Stormbreaker*, the reader feels as if they are a part of the action.

12. Let's go see the movie *Alice in Wonderland*. It's a great movie and Johnny Depp is awesome!

    Is this a valid or invalid argument?
    (Average) (Skill 11.7)

    A. Valid

    B. Invalid

Answer: B. Invaild
The speaker does not offer any support for why they should go and see the movie *Alice in Wonderland* other than the fact that it's a great movie and Johnny Depp is awesome in it.

DIRECTIONS: Read the following passage and answer the questions that follow.

Mr. Smith gave instructions for the painting to be hung on the wall. And then it leaped forth before his eyes: the little cottages on the river, the white clouds floating over the valley, and the green of the towering mountain ranges that were seen in the distance. The painting was so vivid that it seemed almost
real. Mr. Smith was now absolutely certain that the painting had been worth the money.

13. Is this passage biased?
    (Rigorous) (Skill 11.4)

    A. Yes

    B. No

Answer: B. No
The author appears to be simply relating what happened when Mr. Smith had his new painting hung on the wall.

14. From the last sentence, one can infer that:
 (Rigorous) (Skill 11.8)

   A.   The painting was expensive.

   B.   The painting was cheap.

   C.   Mr. Smith was considering purchasing the painting.

   D.   Mr. Smith thought the painting was too expensive and decided not to purchase it.

Answer: A. The painting was expensive
The correct answer is A. Option B is incorrect because, had the painting been cheap, chances are that Mr. Smith would not have considered his purchase.
Options C and D are ruled out by the fact that the painting had already been purchased, as is clear in the phrase "...the painting had been worth the money."

15. Boys are smarter than girls. Is this sentence fact or opinion?
 (Easy) (Skill 11.3)

   A.   Fact

   B.   Opinion

Answer: B. Opinion
There isn't any scientific evidence to back up this idea.

16. Turkey burgers are better than beef burgers. Is this sentence fact or opinion?
 (Easy) (Skill 11.3)

   A.   Fact

   B.   Opinion

Answer: B. Opinion
Those who believe that turkey burgers are better than beef burgers might think this statement is a fact. However, it is not able to be proven and can in fact be argued so therefore, it is an opinion.

17. **Johnny Depp stars in the movie *Charlie and the Chocolate Factory*. Is this sentence fact or opinion?**
    (Easy) (Skill 11.3)

    A.   Fact

    B.   Opinion

Answer: A. Fact
It can be proven that Johnny Depp is the actor who stars in a leading role in *Charlie and the Chocolate Factory*.

18. **We live at 5310 Fair Oaks Drive in Chicago, Illinois. Is this sentence fact or opinion?**
    (Easy) (Skill 11.3)

    A.   Fact

    B.   Opinion

Answer: A. Fact
The address that the author resides at is indisputable and cannot be argued. Therefore, it is a fact.

19. **What conclusion can be drawn from the passage below?**
    (Rigorous) (Skill 11.8)

    When she walked into the room she gasped in disbelief as her hands rose to her face and her eyes bulged large. After she picked her jaw up off the floor, a huge smile spread across her face as her best friend came up and wrapped her arms around her and wished her a happy birthday.

    A.   The girl didn't know anyone in the room

    B.   The girl saw something shocking

    C.   The girl was being thrown a surprise party

    D.   The girl got punched in the face

Answer: C. The girl was being thrown a surprise party
The last sentence of the paragraph solidifies the idea that the girl is being thrown a surprise party for her birthday.

20. What conclusion can be drawn from the paragraph below?
    (Average) (Skill 11.8)

    Joel stood at the water's edge staring into the waves as his legs trembled violently. His mind flashed back to last summer and his entire body joined his legs and began to tremble. He tried to even his breathing as he took slow deep breaths before deciding to head into the surf.

    A. The water was really cold

    B. Joel saw a shark in the water

    C. Last summer was better than this summer

    D. Joel is afraid of the water because something happened

Answer: D. Joel is afraid of the water because something happened
There are many clues that would lead to any of these choices. However, Joel is trembling with fear and thinks back to the summer before because something terrible must have happened.

DIRECTIONS: Read the following passage and answer the questions that follow.

Deciding which animal to get as the family pet can be a very difficult decision, and there are many things to take into consideration. First, you must consider the size of your home and the area that will be dedicated to the pet. If your home is a smaller one, then you probably want to get a small dog or even a cat. If you are lucky enough to have larger home with plenty of room inside and out, then most certainly consider a large or even a more active breed of dog. One other thing to consider is how often and how long you are outside of the home. Cats do not need to be let out to relieve themselves. They are normally trained to use a litter box. On the other hand, dogs require being let out. Dogs also require more exercise than cats and often need to be walked. This can be aggravating to an owner especially on rainy days. Therefore, when deciding which pet is best for your family, it is necessary to consider more than whether or not you want a dog or a cat, but which animal will best fit into your family's lifestyle.

21. How does the author feel about dogs?
(Rigorous) (Skill 11.5)

    A.   The author likes dogs and cats the same

    B.   The author thinks that dogs are aggravating

    C.   The author believes they require more care than cats

    D.   The author feels that dogs are more active than cats

Answer: C. The author believes they require more care than cats
The author gives two examples of things dogs need more than cats. It is stated that dogs require being let out and that they require more exercise.

22. How does the author feel about the size of people's houses?
    (Rigorous) (Skill 11.5)

    A.   The author believes that people with larger homes are lucky

    B.   The author thinks that if you have a small house you should have a cat

    C.   The author feels that only people with large homes should own animals

    D.   The author thinks that only those who own homes should own pets

Answer: A. The author believes that people with larger homes are lucky
Within the passage the author says, "If you are lucky enough to own a large house."

23. From this passage, one can infer that:
    (Rigorous) (Skill 11.8)

    A.   The author owns a cat

    B.   More people own dogs than cats

    C.   Cats are smarter than dogs

    D.   The author owns a dog

Answer: D. The author owns a dog
One sentence in particular gives the reader the idea that the author owns a dog because she says, "This [walking the dog or letting it out] can be aggravating to an owner especially on rainy days."

24. From this passage, one can infer that:
   (Rigorous) (Skill 11.8)

   A. Either a dog or cat will be right for every family who wants a pet

   B. Choosing a pet is not solely one family member's job

   C. Only someone who enjoys exercising should get a dog

   D. Big dogs will not survive in a small house

Answer: B. Choosing a pet is not solely one family member's job
The word "family" is used several times in the article, and therefore, the reader knows that choosing a pet is a family's responsibility—not just one member's.

DIRECTIONS: Read the following passage and answer the questions that follow.

According to Factmonster.com, the most popular Internet activity is sending and/or reading email. Approximately 92% of Internet users report using the Internet for this purpose. 89% of Internet users report that they use the Internet to search for information. Two popular search engines are Google and Yahoo! The introduction of the Internet has made it easy to gather and research information quickly. Other reasons that Internet users use the Internet is to search for driving directions, look into a hobby or interest, or research a product or service before buying, just to name a few. Creative <u>enterprises</u> such as remixing songs or lyrics stood at the bottom of reasons people use the Internet. Surprisingly, only 11% of Internet users said they use the Internet for creative purposes. Perhaps people are using specific software to be creative. Where do you rank? Think about why you last used the Internet.

25. What is the main idea of the passage?
    (Average) (Skill 10.1)

    A. Factmonster has a lot of great facts for people to research

    B. People use the Internet for a variety of reasons

    C. The main reason the Internet is used is to check emails

    D. People aren't as creative as they used to be before the Internet

Answer: B. People use the Internet for a variety of reasons
The passage lists the top reasons why people use the Internet. Therefore, the best choice is B.

26. Why did the author write this article?
    (Average) (Skill 11.1)

    A. To convince the reader to use the Internet

    B. To teach the reader how use the Internet

    C. To encourage the reader to use the Internet

    D. To inform the reader about Internet usage trends

Answer: D. To inform the reader about Internet usage trends
The author wants to let the reader know what the Internet is mostly being used for. The statistics offered are synonymous of Internet usage trends.

27. **How is the passage organized?**
    (Average) (Skill 11.2)

    A. Sequence of events

    B. Cause and effect

    C. Statement support

    D. Compare and contrast

Answer: C. Statement support
The passage makes a statement at the beginning and then supports it with details in the rest of the passage.

28. **What cause and effect relationship exists in this paragraph?**
    (Rigorous) (Skill 11.6)

    A. The U.S. postal service is suffering from the introduction of email

    B. Google and Yahoo! are used most often to search information

    C. The introduction of the Internet has made gathering information easy

    D. People are less creative since they aren't using their computers for this reason

Answer: C. The introduction of the Internet has made gathering information easy
Because the Internet was introduced, people are able to search for information easier than they used to be able to. This is a cause and effect relationship.

29. By using the word "surprisingly" in the passage, what is the author implying?
    (Rigorous) (Skill 10.1)

    A.   It is thought that the Internet is used more for creative purposes

    B.   People are thought to be more creative than they really are

    C.   It is thought that fewer than 11% would use the Internet for creative purposes

    D.   Software companies are making 11% more creative software

Answer: A. It is thought that the Internet is used more for creative purposes
By using the word "surprisingly," the author is saying that she is surprised that only 11% of Internet users use the Internet for creative purposes. The author would expect that number to be higher.

30. Which transition word could the author have used to connect these two sentences?
    (Average) (Skill 10.1)

    Approximately 92% of Internet users report using the Internet for this purpose. 89% of Internet users report that they use the Internet to search for information.

    A.   Additionally,

    B.   Therefore,

    C.   Next,

    D.   Similarly,

Answer: A. Additionally,
The author wants to add more information about Internet usage, so "additionally" is the best choice for a transition word.

31. **What does the word "enterprises" mean in the passage?**
    (Average) (Skill 10.3)

    A. people

    B. endeavors

    C. businesses

    D. musicians

Answer: B. endeavors
The words "endeavors" and "enterprises" are synonymous, and either word could be used in the passage.

DIRECTIONS: Read the following passage and answer the questions that follow.

The poems both use personification to bring the subjects of the poem to life. Both poems were also very entertaining. In "The Subway" the author says that the subway, also known as a dragon, swallows up the people and then spits them out at the next stop. Similarly, in "Steam Shovel," the author says that the steam shovel chews up the dirt that it scoops up and smiles amiably at the people below.
   The subjects of the poems are compared to different things. The subway is compared to a dragon with green scales. Dragons breathe fire. The steam shovel is compared to an ancient dinosaur with a long neck and dripping jaws.

32. **How is the passage organized?**
    (Average) (Skill 11.2)

    A. Compare and contrast

    B. Cause and effect

    C. Sequence of events

    D. Statement support

Answer: A. Compare and contrast
This passage compares (gives similarities) and contrasts (shows differences) between two poems.

33. Which sentence in the passage is irrelevant?
    (Average) (Skill 11.6)

    A. Both poems were also very entertaining.

    B. The subway is also known as a dragon.

    C. The subway swallows people up and spits them out.

    D. The author says that the steam shovel chews up the dirt.

Answer: A. Both poems were also very entertaining.
Although this may be a similarity between the two poems, it is an opinion that is not necessary to include within the passage, since the focus of the first paragraph is personification.

34. Which sentence in the passage is irrelevant?
    (Rigorous) (Skill 11.6)

    A. The subjects of the poems are compared to different things.

    B. The subway is compared to a dragon with green scales.

    C. Dragons breathe fire.

    D. The steam shovel is compared to an ancient dinosaur.

Answer: C. Dragons breathe fire.
Although "dragons breathe fire" is an extension of the idea that the subway is being compared to a dragon with green scales, the idea doesn't quite fit in and isn't necessary.

DIRECTIONS: Read the following passage and answer the questions that follow.

Have you ever wondered what chewing gum is made from? What is it that allows us to chew it for hours without it ever disintegrating? Chicle is a gum, or sap, that comes from the sapodilla tree. The sapodilla tree is an American tropical evergreen that is native to South Florida. Flavorings, corn syrup, and sugar or artificial sweeteners are other ingredients that go into the production of chewing gum. Legend has it that Native Americans chewed spruce resin to quench their thirst. Today, gum is chewed for many reasons by many different groups of people.

35. What conclusion can be drawn from the passage?
   (Rigorous) (Skill 11.8)

   A.   Everyone in South Florida has heard of the sapodilla tree

   B.   Many people have wondered what makes gum chewy

   C.   Some type of sweetener is used in gum production

   D.   Native Americans invented gum

Answer: C. Some type of sweetener is used in gum production
It is defined in the passage that sugar or artificial sweeteners are used in gum production.

36. What can be inferred from the passage?
   (Rigorous) (Skill 11.8)

   A.   The gum Chiclets took its name from the ingredient chicle used in gum

   B.   Gum is disgusting after it's been chewed for a few hours

   C.   Gum is only made in the United States because that's where the sapodilla tree grows

   D.   When someone is thirsty they should chew gum

Answer: A. The gum Chiclets took its name from the ingredient chicle used in gum
It can be inferred from the passage that the brand of gum called Chiclets most likely took its name from the ingredient chicle, or sap, that is found in gum.

DIRECTIONS: Read the following passage and answer the questions that follow.

The word "cycle" comes from the Greek word *kyklos*, which means "circle" or "wheel." There are many different types of cycles. The word "unicycle" comes from the prefix *uni-*, which means "one," combined with the root "cycle." When the prefix and root word cycle are combined, it creates a word that means "one circle or wheel." Unicycles are often used for entertainment rather than exercise.

A prefix *bi-* means "two," which, when combined with the word "cycle," creates the word "bicycle." How many wheels does a bicycle have? Many young children ride a tricycle because it has three wheels and is easy to ride. The prefix *tri-* means "three," and when it is combined with the root word "cycle," the new word is "three wheels." It is even possible to make the word "motorcycle." Once you know how to use roots, it is easy to figure out the meaning of an unknown word.

37. **What is the main idea of the passage?**
    (Average) (Skill 10.1)

    A.   There are many types of cycles

    B.   The prefix *uni-* means one

    C.   Words can be defined by their parts

    D.   Unicycles are often used for entertainment

Answer: C. Words can be defined by their parts
Only Option C covers the whole passage and not just one small detail contained within it.

38. **What does the word "roots" mean?**
    (Easy) (Skill 10.3)

    A.   Stable parts of plants

    B.   Where one originated

    C.   The base portions of a word

    D.   A spelling tool

Answer: C. The base portions of a word
"Roots" is a multiple-meaning word, but in the context of the passage, it means the base portions of a word.

39. Which is an opinion contained in this passage?
    (Average) (Skill 11.3)

    A. Once you know how to use roots, it is easy to figure out the meaning of an unknown word

    B. Many young children ride a tricycle

    C. Unicycles are often used for entertainment rather than exercise

    D. The word "cycle" comes from the Greek word *kyklos*

Answer: A. Once you know how to use roots, it is easy to figure out the meaning of an unknown word
Options B and C could be opinions, but they both have clarifying words like "many" and "often," which makes them facts.

40. From this article you can see that the author thinks:
    (Rigorous) (Skill 10.1)

    A. Riding a bicycle is good exercise

    B. It is important to know about the English language

    C. "Cycle" is a confusing word

    D. It is more important to understand the prefixes and suffixes

Answer: B. It is important to know about the English language
The author wrote this passage to teach readers about the English language. Therefore, we know that the author thinks it is important to understand the English language.

More Study Tools to Help Pass Your Certification Exam

XAMonline.com

Pass your exam with our suite of superior study tools, including:

- Print books
- eBooks
- eFlashcards
- Web-based interactive study guides

Teaching in another state? XAMonline carries 500+ state-specific and PRAXIS study guides covering every test subject nationwide.

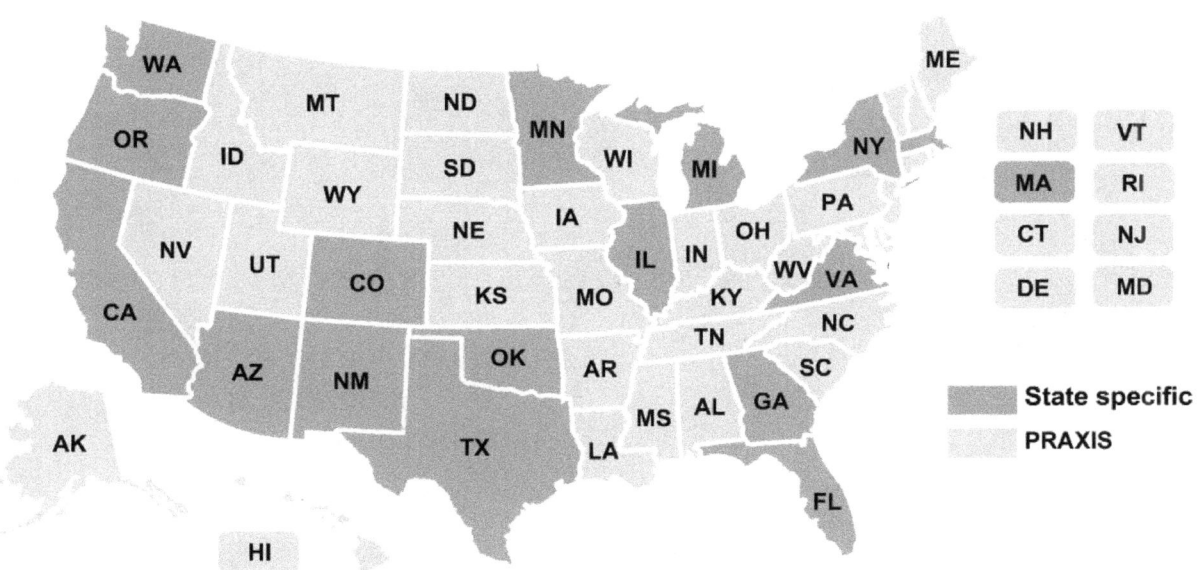

Call or visit us online!
800.301.4647 | www.XAMonline.com

www.ingramcontent.com/pod-product-compliance
Lightning Source LLC
Chambersburg PA
CBHW062128160426
43191CB00013B/2228